HOW TO NEGOTIATE THE RAISE YOU DESERVE

HOW TO NEGOTIATE THE RAISE YOU DESERVE

Mark Satterfield

NEW ENGLAND INSTITUTE
OF TECHNOLOGY
LEARNING RESOURCES CENTER

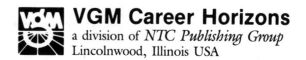 **VGM Career Horizons**
a division of *NTC Publishing Group*
Lincolnwood, Illinois USA

194

#27143870

Library of Congress Cataloging-in-Publication Data

Satterfield, Mark
    How to negotiate the raise you deserve / by Mark Satterfield.

        p.   cm.
    ISBN 0-8442-4168-7 (soft)
    1. Promotions.   2. Negotiation in business.   I. Title.
HF5549.5.P7S23   1993
650.14—dc20   92-41903
                                                        CIP

Published by VGM Career Horizons, a division of NTC Publishing Group.
© 1993 by NTC Publishing Group, 4255 West Touhy Avenue,
Lincolnwood (Chicago), Illinois 60646-1975 U.S.A.
Manufactured in the United States of America.

3 4 5 6 7 8 9 0 VP 9 8 7 6 5 4 3 2 1

Dedication
To my wife, Karen, my partner in all
the important negotiations.

About the
Author

Mark Satterfield is a career consultant, speaker, and columnist for the *Atlanta Constitution*. He was formerly placement director for the MBA program at Emory University and has directed recruiting programs for PepsiCo and Kraft.

Contents

Introduction

Money. Moola. Wampum. Lucre. Green. Bucks. Bread. Dough. Regardless of what you call it, money is a subject of endless fascination. Money is more than just a standard of living. It helps us keep score on how well we are doing in our careers. Unfortunately, despite our interest in the subject, most people take a surprisingly passive approach to their own level of compensation. Whatever the company offers we often feel obliged to accept. We think that salary negotiating is limited to celebrities and other highly compensated individuals. In fact, salary negotiating can, and should be, practiced by virtually everyone.

The problem in trying to get the money you deserve is that most people don't know how to do it. They are afraid of having their request rejected and consequently are afraid to try. People mistakenly believe that their salaries are set in stone. Most often this is not the case.

Not all salaries can be negotiated, however. As a general

rule the more experience you have, and the smaller the company you work for, the greater your flexibility to negotiate salary. A recent college graduate going to work for a bank may find the bank to be inflexible on the starting salary. However, an experienced computer programmer working for a small high-tech firm is likely to discover much room to negotiate. Even the recent graduate may find that the bank is willing to bend on issues such as the amount of vacation given or how frequently the salary is to be reviewed and adjusted. The key is knowing what to ask for.

Salary negotiating is a game, just like any other aspect of business. In order to be successful, you've got to know how the game is played. The skills that you will develop in learning how to be an effective salary negotiator are very helpful in other areas of your life. Once you master these skills, you'll be a better purchaser of services and will feel more self-confident about many aspects of your life.

In order to understand how the game is played, we'll start out with an overview of the principles involved in negotiation. These principles hold true whether you are negotiating for a raise or buying a car. We'll also review how companies determine salaries, and how they arrive at the number they offer you. In order for you to be an effective negotiator, you've got to know what your worth is in the marketplace. It's not as difficult to learn as you might imagine. We'll review the sources of information available to you to ensure that you're not content with too little money.

Many people forget that salaries are only one component of total compensation. There are a lot of other perks you may be able to get, if you only ask. Benefits make up a significant portion of your total compensation package, yet they are commonly misunderstood. If you don't fully understand benefits, it is difficult to compare one company's offer against another's.

The fact that some industries pay better than others won't come as a surprise to most people. What you may not know is where the highest paying jobs are in selected industries and functions. We'll also discuss trends for the 1990s. What can you expect for a salary increase in the years ahead? Since money is also a way of keeping score, I'll provide you with guidelines to determine how you're doing. The antiquated notion that you should be earning $1,000 for each year of age no longer applies. Cost of living is an issue if you are thinking about moving to another area of the country. We'll discuss how to compare similar offers in different cities and how to determine just how expensive a city really is to live in.

Now that we know how salaries are determined and what our market value is, we'll learn how to negotiate. Dispelling some of the misconceptions associated with salary negotiating is an important first step. You'll need to develop specific skills in order to be an effective negotiator, and we'll review practical tips on how to become adept and comfortable with the negotiating process.

Salary negotiating is not about becoming rich overnight. It's also not about getting the best of your employer. As we'll discuss, relatively few employers will intentionally low-ball you on salary. It's simply not good business for them to do so. However, avoiding being intentionally low-balled and maximizing your salary potential are two different things.

We all want to be paid fairly. At a minimum, the advice in this book will help you achieve that goal. However, true salary negotiators want to go beyond simply being paid a competitive wage. They want everything that they have coming to them. That's the goal of this book: to give you the information necessary so that you don't leave money or perks on the table.

Let's proceed.

Fundamentals of Negotiation

People are often intimidated by the prospect of negotiating. They typically think that the process is more complex than it actually is. While there are methods and tactics that the experienced negotiator can use to his or her advantage, anyone can become an effective negotiator. In fact, you probably already negotiate more than you realize. Negotiating successfully depends upon preparation and communication. There is no voodoo, nor is the process so inordinately complex that only a few can master it. Becoming an effective negotiator has mostly to do with wanting to develop the skills necessary for success.

Negotiating is a fundamental element of human behavior. We negotiate all the time; often without realizing that we are doing so. Any time we enter into a conversation with another party in which the goal is to reach agreement, we are negotiating. Sometimes the process is informal and instinctive. Other times it is the culmination of many hours of preparation.

The goal of negotiations is to reach agreement. Individuals who enter the negotiating process intent on complete victory are usually disappointed. Even if victory is achieved, it can come at such a high price that it becomes meaningless.

This is what has occurred at many of the nation's newspapers over the past ten years. Workers went on strike over wages and job security. The negotiations were filled with recriminations and emotions ran high. The workers' leadership was intent on not giving in on any of their demands. After a long and costly battle, the workers' demands were met. But the price the workers paid was high. Many of the newspapers subsequently folded. The battle was won but the war was lost.

When it comes to negotiating salary, one has to be particularly sensitive not to alienate the other party. The relationship between yourself and your prospective employer will, you hope, become a long-term engagement. You can avoid alienating the other party by determining ahead of time exactly what you want to achieve in the negotiation. This preparation is one of the fundamentals to successful negotiations. It's important that you negotiate in order to achieve your goals rather than to simply squeeze the company for every last dime.

As Nicholas Kent recounts in his book *Naked Hollywood* on how talent agents negotiate:

> You've got your basic 'mercy' deal—which is when you throw yourself on the mercy of the other person—to your 'you have all the cards' deal, in which case you just pound the living hell out of the other guy. But remember that you're going to be doing this for a long time. Every time you go out and beat the hell out of somebody, remember that today you own the bat but tomorrow the other guy may own the bat and he's going to beat the hell out of you. Use a velvet glove. It's very important to be liked.

One must take a long-term approach to negotiations. You are likely to have many negotiations with the same people over the years. There is little long-term benefit to developing a reputation as a greedy individual. Remember the old Wall Street maxim: "Bulls make money. Bears make money. Pigs get slaughtered."

Understanding Human Behavior

You need two different types of knowledge in order to be a successful negotiator: knowledge about yourself and knowledge of human behavior. Although human beings are individually complex and hard to predict, the behavior of groups of people is much more predictable. You must become, as Paul Newman's character said in "The Color of Money," a "student of human moves." The more you know about people and what motivates them, the more likely you are to be able to predict how they will react. This knowledge will enable you to predict objections and carefully develop persuasive arguments to overcome the objections. The more you anticipate the issues and practice articulating your rebuttals, the more successful you will become.

A mistake negotiators often make is to assume that people will make rational decisions. "If I explain why my solution is in the best interests of both parties," the negotiator thinks, "they will have no alternative but to agree with me." This argument is true in theory but not in practice. What everyone forgets is that people make decisions with both their heads and their hearts. A peculiar combination of reason and emotion is employed in making decisions. Although the logic to your argument is sound, it may lose to a purely emotional reaction by the other party. For example, what you are saying may sometimes be clouded by how you look. You may remind your opponent of his ex-wife, brother, or best friend. Or the fact that your shoes aren't shined may cause the other person to think negatively about you. Your success in negotiating will depend on a variety of factors. While your argument cannot be illogical, reason by itself will not necessarily sway the person to your point of view.

Our negotiating skills will become enhanced the more we understand human behavior. Although we do not need to become psychologists in order to become effective negotiators, understanding some of the psychological traits that influence human behavior can be helpful.

Rationalization

For example, the power of rationalization can often be used to our advantage. We rationalize things in our minds all the time. It is our mind's method of helping us cope when we don't get our way. If we can't rationalize something we usually resist it tooth and nail. We are far more likely to accept a less than perfect outcome if we can somehow justify it. Rationalization is a powerful trait of human behavior that can help or hurt us in a negotiation.

Rationalization can make us too willing to give in. If our opponent can give us a justification for why we should bend to their will, it may be tempting to do so. This is particularly appealing if the negotiation has been going on for some time. Negotiating is like any other activity that requires concentration and mental alertness. After a while, one simply gets tired. While we are adamant in the initial stages, as the hours drag on we begin to seek any reason to end the negotiation. Concluding the discussion becomes preferable to making the best possible deal. It is very easy at this stage to fall prey to rationalizing our lack of success.

For example, a common objection you're likely to hear during salary negotiating is, "You're asking for more money than we're paying people who already work here." This is a blatant attempt by your opponent to get you to rationalize accepting less money. "Oh well, I certainly can't justify being paid more than experienced workers." In this case the power of rationalization has worked against you.

However, rationalization can also be a powerful tool to help you achieve your objectives. Remember, you must provide your opponent a justification for why your solution is the preferred outcome. "I understand your concern, Mr. Employer," you might reply. "However, as you will recall, I do have a graduate degree in this field, which I don't believe anybody on your current staff has, and I have worked five years for your major competitor on similar issues." This is your rationalization or justification for why you should be paid more money. In order to be successful, however, you must anticipate the objection and prepare your justification. Preparation and justification are two important fundamental weapons to successful negotiations.

Projection   Another element of human behavior which we can use to our advantage is what the psychologists refer to as "projection"; that is, assuming other people are motivated by the same things we are. Even though logic would dictate otherwise, we tend to think that everyone desires the same things that we do. Again, we can use this element of human behavior to our advantage.

In order to capitalize on this weakness you must be very alert for clues. You must first determine what your opponent thinks is important. It is likely to be easier to negotiate with your opponent on the issues that he or she doesn't think are as valuable. Be alert for signals. Repeatedly stressing a particular point is often a tip-off to something that is quite important to the person. Your opponent may erroneously think that this is equally important to you. This can provide you with some unique room to negotiate.

For example, say that in your conversation the manager repeatedly stresses the bonus program. You *can* conclude that money is a prime motivator for this person. It's likely that he thinks it's very important to you, also. You need to think about the other components of the compensation program that the manager didn't mention. He probably puts little value on those pieces. For example, he may be surprisingly accommodating to giving you more vacation time. In his mind, vacations are a distant second to bonuses; thus, they have less value and are more easily given away. The more you understand human behavior, the more options you will have.

Understanding Yourself

The second type of knowledge you need in order to be a successful negotiator is self-knowledge. It's surprising how many people enter into a negotiation without a clear sense of what they want to achieve. It's like going on a trip without a map. You're bound to wind up somewhere, but it may not be a place where you wanted to be.

Unfortunately, many people go into negotiations armed only with the vague sense that they want to strike a "good deal." What exactly would constitute a good deal has not been thought through. A common example of such a situation is when people go to buy a car. They enter the dealer's showroom knowing only that they don't want to pay the sticker price. They often are not certain of what they do want to pay, or what they can even afford. They are easy prey for the shrewd salesman who speaks in terms of monthly payments rather than total price. It's no wonder that few people really feel as if they got a truly good deal and dread the process of having to buy another car.

Spending time preparing for any negotiation is crucial for success. You've got to invest the time to evaluate what you want to accomplish in the meeting. What is more important for you to achieve? What are you willing to compromise on? What's your minimum requirement? All of these questions need to be determined in advance. Otherwise, when it's all over, you'll have no idea whether you struck a good, fair, or poor deal.

When you're preparing to negotiate your compensation package, think about what your work means to you. Is it one of your primary sources of satisfaction or is it simply a means to finance the things that are important to you? Some of us are very motivated by money. For one person the salary, stock options, and bonus plans are the most important negotiating points.

However, just because one person is motivated by money, you needn't be motivated by the same thing. Ironically, people often fervently negotiate for things they don't even want, or for things they think should be important, but in fact really aren't. For instance, some people have "jobs," while others have "careers." The fundamental difference between the two is that people with careers tend to put their word first while people with jobs get their primary satisfaction from other parts of their life, such as family, church, or leisure activities. There's nothing wrong with either. However, it is important to know which you have before you enter into the negotiation.

If in your heart of hearts you know that your job only serves to finance the other activities that are most important to you in life, money isn't going to be a major motivator for you. Sure, you would always like to have more money, but you don't absolutely need the extra income. You might be willing to settle for a little less money if you could get a little more vacation. If you're this type of person, working for a college or university might be an ideal career move. Academia doesn't tend to pay a lot of money, but it does tend to be quite generous with vacations.

However, it's unlikely that you will be able to focus on negotiating the right issues or apply for the right kinds of jobs if you don't know what it is that's important to you. Without preparation, you will face difficulty in arriving at a deal that is truly satisfactory and best meets your personal needs.

Negotiation is all about preparation and knowledge of human behavior. In order to be a successful negotiator, all you really need is a desire to develop the skills you need, some common sense, and a willingness to invest time in preparation before the meeting. We'll discuss each of these fundamentals of negotiation in more detail in subsequent chapters.

Future Trends

Everyone is always interested in the future. What trends are likely to occur that we can capitalize on? Although trends are difficult to predict, if you are ahead of the curve you can reap enormous benefits. For example, being aware of changes in compensation can help you compare offers and make sure you are not overlooking anything. Companies are often willing to provide you with additional perks if you remember to ask for them. However, companies often don't like to set a precedent for new compensation arrangements. Statements such as "We've never done that before" are common when the company doesn't want to break precedent. However, if you understand current trends in compensation, you can bolster your argument by discussing the historical precedent for what you are asking.

In order to understand what's changing in the world of compensation, it's important that you fully understand all of the components that make up your compensation package. If you don't know the value of everything currently being provided to you, you're at a disadvantage in negotiating.

For example, far too often we become fixated on salaries. We define how much we "make" by this amount. Equating salaries with total compensation minimizes our total worth. Although salary makes up the bulk of our compensation when we are in the junior and middle management ranks, this becomes no longer true as we progress up the ladder.

✓ **Benefits**

Even at the most junior level, the benefit plan may add an additional 20 to 30 percent to the base salary. When thinking about total compensation, you must also consider such factors as disability insurance, paid vacations, educational opportunities, child care assistance, stock options, profit sharing, and retirement programs. If you are to successfully negotiate, you must fully appreciate and understand the value of each of these components. Since many companies provide little information on many of these factors, we can easily forget that they are worth a great deal of money. If, for example, your company provides child care assistance, think about how much that would cost you out of pocket if you had to pay for it yourself. Suddenly that new offer paying $100 more per week but not including any child care benefits doesn't look as attractive. It is up to us to take the initiative to make sure we fully understand the dollar value of each of these programs.

One trend affecting compensation revolves around health insurance. One of the largest and fastest growing costs facing employers is health care. Twenty years ago many companies picked up the full cost of health care insurance premiums. Today it is rare to find an employer so generous. As health care costs have escalated, companies have increased the amount of the contribution each employee must pay.

A standard Blue Cross/Blue Shield major medical plan for you and your spouse has a monthly premium today of approximately $350. Years ago, when the premium was much smaller, the company often picked up the entire tab. Today a "good" health care program may only pick up 50 percent of the premium. In this program you would pay $150 just to provide health care coverage for your family.

As insurance premiums rise, the trend is toward "managed health care" programs. Under these programs, only treatments by pre-approved physicians are covered. Naturally, these programs have met with a great deal of controversy. These programs run contrary to the perceived right of people to find their own doctors. As much as you may not like it, managed health care programs are the trend for the future. Thus, a benefit program in which the entire premium is paid by your employer, or which allows you to select the physician of your choice, becomes a more valuable component of the compensation mix than perhaps you originally thought. The trend in health care coverage is certainly one that you will want to keep current on as you anticipate negotiating your compensation package in the future.

You may not realize that insurance and retirement programs are a relatively new phenomenon. Until the 1930s you were responsible for your own health care coverage. If you didn't save enough to ensure a certain standard of living in your old age, it was considered to be your own fault. The Social Security Act of 1935 changed this perception forever. The responsibility for maintaining an adequate lifestyle in the later years shifted from the individual to the government and employers. As more and more employees participated in health care and retirement programs, the cost to the individual employee was dramatically reduced.

Interestingly, in the past forty years the cost of benefits has risen much faster than salaries. Thus, your benefits make up a significantly larger percentage of your total compensation package than they did forty years ago. Unfortunately, many workers take their benefits for granted and don't think of them as a part of compensation. However, as companies scramble to cut costs in the 1990s, benefit packages will vary significantly from company to company.

The transformation of benefits from nonexistent to taken for granted is credited largely to the labor union movement of the 1930s and 1940s. During the peak of America's union membership, unions were successful in accelerating both wages and benefits. Although only 16 percent of today's work force is unionized, their legacy of benefit coverage for workers remains.

The whole concept of benefits has changed in the past ten years, and the trend toward change is accelerating rapidly. Historically benefit programs were structured on the assumption that one spouse worked and the other stayed at home raising the family. The reality has changed dramatically. The typical American home in the 1990s usually has two wage earners. Thus, the need for comprehensive benefits, which are designed to cover the entire family, becomes a somewhat antiquated notion. In response to these changes, an increasing number of companies are implementing flexible benefit programs. Employees select from a menu of benefits the ones that are the most valuable to them, thereby tailoring their benefit programs to their lifestyle and family status. Some companies are even providing workers with a dollar figure that can be used to purchase benefits. The employee not needing benefits can elect to have the money added to his or her paycheck. It is likely that we will see more of these programs in the future.

What else might we expect in the future?

Pay for Performance

The concept of pay for performance has received much attention recently. It's hard to fault it. Top performers should receive larger raises than marginal performers. But it's easier said than done. Although it sounds good in theory, actually implementing a "pay for performance" program is enormously difficult. Despite the press it receives, American businesses aren't any closer to actually paying for performance than they were twenty years ago.

Salary increases are most likely to continue as they have in the past. You can expect that your merit increase will largely be a reflection of the inflation rate. Two or three percentage points will separate the stars from the drones. Unfortunately, a true pay for performance program tends to upset the majority of people who don't get the large increase. The problem is magnified since most companies don't have effective performance appraisal systems in place. Thus, the process breaks down into quarrelsome factions, each advocating its own employees. In frustration, companies throw up their hands and try to keep everyone "whole" by tying salary raises to inflation. Unless you are promoted, your level of buying power is likely to remain flat.

Although annual raises will probably remain almost the same for top- and middle-level performers, companies will have to reward top workers if they expect to keep them. Increasingly, the answer to this problem is participation in the incentive bonus plan. More companies are expanding the level and number of workers who participate. In certain industries, such as the financial companies on Wall Street, the annual bonus makes up the overwhelming majority of one's pay. While bonuses help increase the fairness of the compensation system, an individual's income level can change dramatically from year to year.

Declining Role of Unions

Union clout has been waning for the past two decades. As American manufacturing shifted first to the southern part of the United States and then overseas, union power continued to diminish. The organizational restructurings that affected virtually every area of business in the late 1980s caused job security to be more important than wages for many workers. The trend for the unionized work force is to accept lower hourly wages and cuts in benefits for increased job security.

Increased Differences Between Occupations and Educational Levels

We all know that certain industries pay better than others and that certain jobs within those industries yield the biggest paychecks. In the 1990s, the gap between the highest and lowest paying jobs is likely to widen. While the gap between high school– and college-educated workers has shrunk in the past ten years, the gap between undergraduate and graduate degree holders continues to widen.

Technical schools and associate degree programs have been successful in training individuals for well paying positions in the crafts, computers, and other technical fields. This has largely accounted for the shrinkage of the gap between salaries for high school or trade school graduates and salaries for four-year college graduates.

A master's degree, particularly in a technical field, is still a good investment. The glut of MBAs on the market underscores the importance of specific rather than general expertise at the graduate level. Starting salaries for individuals with graduate degrees in the engineering and computer science fields currently exceed $40,000.

The Perceived Labor Shortage

Much has been written about the work force in the year 2000. The supposition was that the dearth of babies following the baby boom generation would cause a significant labor shortage. This premise has been the rallying cry in the past decade for companies to increase their recruitment of women and minorities in order to make up for the anticipated shortfall in white male workers.

The shortage of workers was expected to have a dramatic impact on salaries, which would have to rise if companies were going to successfully attract this smaller group of talent. These fears lead to concerns that higher salaries would cause inflation to rise, which in turn would put increased upward pressure on raises until the whole compensation-inflation cycle spiraled upward out of control.

It now appears that the prognostications are wrong. Although there will be a labor shortage that will continue into the year 2000, as defined by the numbers of new people entering the work force in the 1990s, it is unlikely that this will have any major affect on wages. The greatest number of job openings are at the very bottom of the wage scale. For example, some of the occupations that are in the greatest need for workers are positions as maids, cooks, delivery people, and other low-skill, low-paying occupations.

Although there will be fewer new workers entering the work force, the glut of middle managers who continue to be laid off is likely to remain. With few middle management slots available, there should be no shortage of talent to fill those positions. Until this bulge of displaced executives find jobs, there will be no upward pressure on salaries.

Temporary Workers

Corporations are likely in the future to be structured around a core group of managers. These individuals will tend to be generalists rather than specialists. Specific expertise will increasingly be purchased from the outside as entire functions are outsourced to specialized consultants.

If a national health care program is implemented, we can expect to see this trend accelerate. Many workers are currently remaining in their jobs primarily because of health benefits that they cannot afford to give up. A national health care program would remove this shackle. The increased use of consultants is a sensible strategy for companies seeking to reduce their fixed expenses. As long as outside vendors can provide services for less than it would cost to keep the function internally, this trend is likely to continue.

Knowing about trends in business is important if you're going to negotiate the best deal possible.

Determining Your Market Value

One of the first problems salary negotiators face is determining market value. It's very difficult to negotiate if you don't know what you're worth. Obtaining this information can sometimes be difficult. Many times our co-workers are reluctant to discuss with us what they are making. Although there is more open discussion about salaries today than in the past, it's a subject many are uncomfortable talking about with friends and associates.

Although you may be uncertain about how to determine your market value, the investment is well worth the effort. A job search can eat up a great amount of time. You can spend fruitless hours pursuing a job only to discover at the final hour that the salary is well below your minimum. Take the time early in your job search to establish your market value. You will then be able to productively focus your time on those jobs that meet your financial requirements.

Where You Fit in the Organization

The first step is to determine where you fit in the organization. If you have just graduated from school or are changing career fields, you'll most likely be applying for an entry-level position. Most entry level jobs pay less than $25,000, although there are exceptions where demand exceeds supply. For example certain entry-level engineering jobs pay up to $35,000.

Middle management jobs often can be identified by the title of Supervisor or Manager. The title of Director usually indicates that one has begun to ascend the upper middle management ranks. Vice-President connotes the beginning of the senior management. However, there is a great deal of flexibility to the weight of titles, depending upon the industry you're in.

In some fields, such as banking, almost everyone is a vice-president. Conversely, in other industries relatively few people hold the title of vice-president. In these organizations the position carries with it considerable clout and responsibility.

Compensation is the purest method of determining where you are in the organization. As a general rule, you're in middle management if you earn between $40,000 and $90,000, and in senior management if you earn $150,000 or more.

The higher you go in the organization, the more your compensation will consist of many different components. In addition to a base salary, you may receive a bonus based on a percentage of your salary, stock options, and other perks. For example, a survey of senior level managers conducted by *Business Week* magazine in 1991 showed that 17 percent of executives could use the company plane, 30 percent were provided with a car phone, 44 percent had reserved parking, 28 percent belonged to a private dining club, and 35 percent had their country club dues picked up by their employer.

Your market value will depend upon a variety of factors. Some of these are easy for you to determine and others are much more difficult. Most companies want to pay the going rate—no more, no less. They don't want to foster the image of being either cheap or spendthrift. Ideally, they want salaries to be a non-issue. They don't want money to be the reason you took or turned down the job.

The factors that go into determining your value will be: (1) how much current employees earn, (2) what similar positions in your industry and region pay, and (3) external forces that impact the supply and demand for talent.

Know What the Company Pays

If current internal employees earn less than what you want to make, your bargaining position is more difficult. The company will have to make an exception if they are going to meet your needs. Although they don't like to admit it, employers make these exceptions on a regular basis. The trick to getting an employer to do the same for you is to convince them that you have skills and capabilities beyond what they currently possess on staff. In other words, you have to convince them of your value. Employers are willing to make exceptions to the rules, but they have to be sold on the idea. Thus, your interviewing skills are extremely important to the salary negotiating process. This is one of the major differences that separates successful negotiators from the also-rans. (We'll discuss this subject in some detail in a later chapter.)

Learning what a company is currently paying its employees is difficult to do unless you personally know people in the organization. However, there are some signs and clues you should be aware of that can help you determine how willing the company may be to make exceptions to their salary structure.

Companies experiencing a period of transition are often most interested in recruiting the best people possible. These corporations are willing to pay whatever it takes to bring talented people on board. Ironically, these companies often are also in the process of laying off other employees. As these companies have become increasingly complex, and as business has changed over time, these companies have found that they often need employees with new or different skills. Unfortunately, current employees may possess skills that have become obsolete, while a shortage exists of individuals with the necessary background and experience.

You can identify these types of companies by being aware of what's going on in business. One trait of most successful senior level executives is that they are voracious readers. They are fascinated with the world of business and make a habit of reading extensively about trends in their industry, and also about what is going on in business in general. They know that a trend which starts in one industry often can be exported to another industry.

At a minimum, you'll want to read the *Wall Street Journal* on a daily basis. You should also subscribe to one or two of the weekly general business magazines. Sample a few copies of either *Forbes, Fortune,* or *Business Week.* Also keep your finger on the pulse of what's going on in your local market by religiously reading the business section of your city's newspaper and by subscribing to your city's business journal. Be on the lookout for newspaper and journal articles that emphasize new initiatives a company is taking. Whenever there is change, there is opportunity. If you have the skills the company needs, they are very likely to pay you a premium dollar for your services.

Conversely, don't pay a lot of attention to national statistics. The media loves to emphasize figures such as housing starts and unemployment rates. While it's always important to know how the nation's economy as a whole is doing, don't forget that you don't live in the whole nation. You live in one town, work in one industry, and perform a very specific task. When statistics come out that focus on you, pay attention. Otherwise, take the information with a grain of salt. By focusing on companies in transition, you may be able to identify some high-paying opportunities and encounter less competition for these jobs. Most people are adverse to risk. They read about layoffs in a particular industry and assume that the company isn't hiring anyone. They are usually wrong.

Another method to identify companies willing to pay top dollar is to remember that these organizations tend to do so consistently throughout the company. They pay top dollar for senior managers, middle managers, and fresh recruits out of college. Check with the placement director at your local college or university. Ask this person which companies have the reputation for paying the largest starting salaries. Identify the most aggressive employers who recruit on campus each year. Which firms compete the hardest for the top students? Which companies will pay whatever it takes? These are the companies with whom you will be most effective in negotiating a salary above the norm.

Knowing Your Market Value

Knowing who your best prospects are is one thing. Knowing your market value is another. You've got to know your worth before you enter the negotiating battle. Fortunately, there are a number of resources available that can help. Most of them are available in either your public library or by mail.

The Bureau of Labor Statistics publishes quarterly reports on salaries in a wide variety of fields. Information is provided by region and nationwide. The Labor Department's *Monthly Labor Review* also provides a summary of this salary information. Most large public libraries keep a copy of these reports.

20

One of the most effective methods to learn your market value is through one of the over three thousand trade and professional associations that exist serving virtually every career field. Becoming a member of a professional association is often overlooked by salary negotiators but can be enormously beneficial.

In addition to the networking benefits, most associations publish an annual survey of their membership. These surveys are usually quite detailed and break out salaries by job title, function, and years of experience. You'll want to join the association that specializes in your functional area (i.e., accounting, sales, human resources, computer science) and in your industry (high technology, consumer goods, automotive, utilities). By joining both types of groups you can be confident that you are obtaining the maximum amount of information about what jobs pay in your field.

An equally valuable resource is recruiting agencies and executive search firms. All professionals, managers, and technicians should make it a point to cultivate a relationship with one or two recruiters who specialize in their field. Recruiters make their living by keeping their finger on the pulse of what's going on. Most of them specialize in a specific field and can serve as a great resource on salary information. However, you've got to invest time to establish a relationship with a recruiter. You won't get much valuable information by just calling up a recruiter cold and asking how much jobs pay in your field.

The best method for establishing a relationship is to be receptive when you get a call from a recruiter. Search professionals are constantly on the phone, seeking information about openings and people. The next time you get such a call, make sure you return it quickly and try to be of help. If you know someone who might be qualified for the position the recruiter represents, provide a referral. Recruiters remember who was helpful and who rushed them off the phone. In this day and age of economic and job insecurity, establishing a relationship with the right recruiter can pay enormous dividends down the road.

Finding recruiters who specialize in your field is easy. *The Directory of Executive Recruiters*, published by Kennedy and Kennedy Publishing in Fitzwilliam, New Hampshire, is the acknowledged bible of recruiters. In this book you'll be able to find recruiters who specialize in your field, industry, and salary level. You'll find that recruiters will be candid with you about your salary expectations. They can often be exactly the resource you need in order to price yourself competitively. We'll discuss further how recruiters can help you in the salary negotiating process in a later chapter.

The importance of researching your market value cannot be overstated. Fortunately, the resources necessary to accurately assess your market worth are readily available. Make sure you take advantage of them.

Why Most Companies Make Fair Offers

One of the problems associated with salary negotiation is that many people think of it as an adversarial relationship. We often assume that if the company can get away with paying us less than we are worth, they probably will. This makes us very skeptical about the company's intentions and clouds the bargaining relationship.

Thus, it may come as a surprise to learn that most companies won't intentionally low-ball on their offer. Certainly there are companies who will try to take advantage of you; however, the number is surprisingly low. Most companies want to pay you a fair wage. Their offer will be based on the type of work you'll be performing, the area of the country in which you're located, and the industry in which you work. Employers ideally want the subject of salary to be a non-issue. They don't want money to be the reason why you accept or turn down the job. How companies determine a fair wage is a subject we'll discuss shortly.

The Painful Process of Recruitment

The primary reason a company will not intentionally give you an artificially low salary offer is that it is not in their best interests to do so. There is a fundamental pragmatic business reason for employers to play fair with you.

Think for a moment about the process of hiring a new employee. Readers who have experienced this know how difficult recruiting can be. Since it's impossible to predict when and who might leave the organization, it's equally impossible to stockpile a group of promising candidates. The process of finding a departing employee's replacement must begin from scratch. Sometimes this process is easy— an employee can be promoted or transferred internally. Often, however, positions aren't filled this painlessly. The company discovers that it must look outside to find a replacement.

Hiring a new person externally is an enormously expensive and time-consuming task. Ads need to be run in the newspaper, which is expensive and tends to generate an enormous number of responses. In addition to the cost of running the ad, someone must spend time sorting through the resumes. Since virtually everyone today knows how to put together an impressive-looking resume, a large number of candidates will need to be personally interviewed in order to narrow the field down to a manageable number. If the ad draws only quantity and not quality, recruiting firms are often brought in to identify candidates. This only adds to the costs.

Making the process even more tiresome is the fact that the departing employee's work must *get done* by someone. Since everyone has more than enough on their plate to begin with, the extra work usually serves to increase tensions within the department. It may even have the effect of causing more employees to quit. Since it takes companies an average of three months to fill professional and managerial openings, the effect of a single key person's departure can be substantial.

Fear of Turnover

Finally, after many months of searching, the right person is found. The individual appears to have the perfect background. She is as enthusiastic about the opportunity as you, the employer, are about having her join your team. The hard work, frustrations, and expense seem to be finally paying off. You make the salary offer, which is accepted, and the new employee begins work.

At this point in time, what is the company's greatest

fear? After a considerable investment of time and money has been made to hire someone, she may not stay. She may quit. No company can completely eliminate turnover; nevertheless, there is one method by which a company will most certainly keep their turnover percentage high: paying an employee a salary below the going market rate. No other factor is more likely to distract workers from performing their tasks, or eventually cause them to quit, than learning that they are being paid less than a similar worker down the street.

Many companies make the erroneous assumption that since people are still reluctant to talk about their salaries, low-paid employees will never find out the truth about *their* status. Employers are both right and wrong about this issue. It is true that many individuals are still reluctant to discuss how much they make. Many won't even discuss the subject with close business associates. However, another force is at work in the marketplace which ensures that if you significantly low-ball an employee, sooner or later they are almost guaranteed to find out: management recruiters.

Management recruiters have emerged in the past twenty years as the arbiters of fairness in salaries. Sooner or later, virtually any professional, technical, senior administrative, or managerial worker will be contacted by a headhunter who specializes in their area of work. In the course of the conversation, the subject of salaries is bound to come up. If an employee is unfairly compensated, the headhunter's pulse quickens. It is an easy matter for the recruiter to sow the seeds of discontent. It is then only a matter of time before the employee has secured new employment, courtesy of the recruiter. The company is once again faced with the expensive and frustrating task of hiring a new person.

Thus, it is simply not in the best interest of the company to intentionally low-ball your salary offer. Most employers want you to be fairly paid, just as they themselves want to be treated in a similar fashion. While you can't expect that an employer is going to overpay you, expecting a fair offer is a realistic expectation which is usually fulfilled. Salary negotiating is a much more pleasant task when you can approach it with a win-win attitude.

What You Should Be Earning

According to the old measure, you were considered on the fast track if you were earning a thousand dollars for each year of age. As with most old measures, it was accurate at one time. However, times moves on. When inflation is factored into the formula, we quickly discover that the old method of computing how well we're doing financially has little or no relevance. Unfortunately, since no nice neat formula has come to replace the measure of $1,000 per year, we're sometimes at a loss as to the best method for determining how *we are* doing.

In fact, the $1,000-per-year rule never had any real significance except to make some of us feel good and some of us feel lousy. The issue isn't how much money you are making in absolute terms. What makes you feel good or bad is how you're doing compared to your direct competition.

For example, a schoolteacher earning $38,000 would feel very good. To get to that level of earnings, the teacher would have had to be consistently rewarded with maximum increases at each raise. However, what makes the teacher feel good could make a worker in a different industry feel terrible. That same $38,000 would be a rounding error for a Wall Street investment banker two to five years out of graduate school. For this small group, earning a compensation package with less than six figures in it is considered less than fast track.

Money doesn't always mean prestige. There are some professions, such as medicine, where they go hand in hand. However, there are many fields in which you can make a killing but which don't rank high on the prestige meter. For example, remember all those kids who went the vocational-technical route in high school? If you think they are all living in duplexes without air conditioning and eating Spam, you obviously haven't needed a plumber recently.

You should feel very good if your annual raise comes in at 7 to 8 percent. As long as inflation remains moderate, the standard raise for the good but not exceptional employee has been 4 to 5 percent. This trend is expected to continue for the next few years.

Salary success varies enormously depending upon your chosen profession, years of experience, and even the region of the country you live in. There are a variety of resources you can use to determine whether you are on the fast track. Two of the most helpful are professional and trade associations and executive recruiters. There are also many salary surveys published each year about specific fields. What follows is a general overview of what a number of career experts believe are reasonable salary expectations for an individual progressing at a respectable pace.

Salary Prospects

Accounting (Major public accounting firm)

Entry level	$ 26,000
Five years	$ 32,000
Ten years	$ 37,000
Twenty years	$ 56,000

Banking/Finance

Entry level	$ 30,000
Five years	$ 38,000
Ten years	$ 45,000
Twenty years	$ 69,000

Civil Service

Entry level	$ 17,000
Five years	$ 26,000
Ten years	$ 32,000
Twenty years	$ 45,000

Computer Programmer

Entry level	$ 27,000
Five years	$ 35,000
Ten years	$ 41,000
Twenty years	$ 56,000

Corporate Law (General counsel for a corporation)

Entry level	A general counsel's position requires 1–3 years of law firm experience.
Five years	$ 57,000
Ten years	$ 64,000
Twenty years	$171,000

Engineering (Overall averages—all disciplines)

Entry level	$ 31,000
Five years	$ 35,000
Ten years	$ 41,000
Twenty years	$ 57,000

Hospitality/Hotel Management

Entry level	$ 22,000
Five years	$ 24,000
Ten years	$ 27,000
Twenty years	$ 55,000

Human Resources

Entry level	$ 27,000
Five years	$ 38,000
Ten years	$ 48,000
Twenty years	$ 65,000

Plumbing

Entry level	$ 25,500
Five years	$ 35,000
Ten years	$ 48,000
Twenty years	$ 75,000

Public Relations

Entry level	$ 28,000
Five years	$ 35,000
Ten years	$ 43,000
Twenty years	$ 65,000

Sales (Industrial products)

Entry level	$ 37,500
Five years	$ 46,000
Ten years	$ 55,000
Twenty years	$ 85,000

Sales (Services)

Entry level	$ 37,000
Five years	$ 43,000
Ten years	$ 49,000
Twenty years	$ 80,000

U.S. Army (Officer)

Entry level	$ 17,500
Five years	$ 22,000
Ten years	$ 32,000
Twenty years	$ 40,500

Presenting Your Salary History

One of the more common and frustrating dilemmas facing salary negotiators is dealing with salary history. This is especially troublesome if we earn a lower than average wage or are attempting to change fields. For example, teaching is a profession that provides great amounts of intangible rewards, but modest pay. Teachers seeking to move into other fields often find themselves hamstrung by their historically low salaries. They find themselves at a competitive disadvantage. Overcoming a low past earnings history is critical if you are to maximize your earnings potential.

Explaining Your Salary History

Your past salary history is important to the process of salary negotiating in a number of ways. First, employers will often benchmark their offer based on your previous earnings—

regardless of your potential. Second, employers view your past earnings as a predictor of your current marketability. A low salary, even in a low-paying industry, can hurt the perception your prospective employer will have of you. Employers are often extremely reluctant to offer you more than a 15 percent increase if they are recruiting you from outside the company. If you were only earning $25,000 in your last job, 15 percent doesn't amount to a large increase.

Certainly there are individuals who are offered more than 15 percent increases to change jobs. These cases are often well documented in the business media. An unfortunate by-product of this coverage is that we can feel inadequate if we aren't successful in negotiating a 30–100 percent jump in salary. From a practical standpoint, these major compensation jumps usually are limited to individuals with specific skills that are in great demand. On average, you should feel good if you receive an offer 15 percent above your current salary. Anything above that should be considered icing on the cake.

There's a lot at stake in this situation. You're justifiably concerned that you may be penalized financially because of your earnings history. Yet you know that you will be asked about what you made in your previous job. At this stage of the game you have three options.

Total Honesty

Your first option is to be completely honest and spell out your weekly, monthly, or annual income. If you're like most people, this will be the most comfortable option for you. Discussing your salary in these terms is the most honest way to handle the question—and the least bright. While the confession may be good for your soul, it will do little for you pocketbook.

Discussing your level of compensation in this manner reveals you at your monetary worst. Ideally, the corporation would take pity on you and immediately offer to correct your financial plight. Practically, your honesty is unlikely to be rewarded. The company is far more likely to view your salary history as an indicator of your worth. Thus, they will offer you a modest increase over what you were making previously in their desire to be fair with you. In theory, everyone is happy—the company probably more so than you.

Outright Fraud

If the completely honest, yet naive, approach doesn't seem to be viable, many people are tempted by the approach of outright fraud. It is often justified by the belief that "ev-

eryone lies a little bit about their salary, so I should, too."
The advantage of lying is that you can dramatically improve your salary history to whatever level you think appropriate. You can also embellish your accomplishments
and achievements to justify your lofty salary success.

The problem with this strategy is that your salary history is so easy to check. Companies who are loath to provide any personal reference information on their employees are usually very happy to verify salary information.
Consider what might happen if your prospective employer
made the following phone call: "Hello, this is Bertrand
Strung from Eny-Miny-Mino-Moe. We're considering offering one of your former employees, Mildred Pierce, a job
with our firm. She states that she earned $125,000 last
year with your company. Can you confirm that?" Whoops!

Calculated Disclosure   If both total honesty and outright fraud don't seem to be
the answer, how does one overcome a low salary history?
The solution lies in truthful, calculated, self-interested disclosure. This can take many forms.

First, think in terms of total compensation rather than
just straight salary. As more and more companies are moving to flexible benefit programs, employees are increasingly being offered the option of purchasing benefits or receiving additional money in their paycheck.

However, you say, the company I'm interviewing with
probably has a benefit program, too. Aren't benefit programs just a wash? Perhaps in the past, but no longer.
Benefits are one of the most expensive components of compensation. Health care costs are rising faster than any
other single expense for employers. Don't kid yourself. The
company you're interviewing with has thought long and
hard about the role benefits play in total compensation.
For example, if you balk at a low salary offer, the company
will be quick to remind you of its excellent benefit program. They are thinking about total compensation and you
should be too.

As benefit costs have continued to escalate, it's rare to
find a company that hasn't put a dollar cost on its benefit
programs. As a general rule most companies pay an additional 20 to 30 percent in benefits for each employee.
That's over and above the salary. Thus, a more accurate
picture of your total compensation would include this percentage.

Another mistake people often make when discussing
their salary is to speak in the past or present tense, rather

than the future. People have a tendency to talk about how much they made, rather than how much they will be making in the near future. You can penalize yourself thousands of dollars by doing this.

Say that it's August and you are interviewing for a new job. You're currently earning $30,000 per year. Your review date with your current employer is in September. Since your boss has indicated you're doing a good job you could reasonable expect a salary increase in the 6 to 8 percent range. A mistake many job changers make is that when asked how much they are earning, they answer $30,000. They are talking about their current income, rather than what they will be making in a month. This automatically pushes their bargaining position back by 6 to 8 percent.

Always speak in terms of what you expect to make in the current year. If a salary review is scheduled for less than six months in the future, discuss your salary in terms of what you'll be earning after the merit increase. Don't shortchange yourself out of the commendable (but foolish) desire to be perfectly and completely honest.

Also, don't forget to factor in unique perks or benefits. In many universities, employees can participate in a "courtesy scholarship" program, which enables them to send their children to the college for free. This benefit can be worth over $20,000! If you're a university employee, this might be an important part of your compensation package.

What about retirement programs? They are not all the same. Teachers, particularly those who work in colleges or universities, belong to a program in which for every dollar they contribute, the company puts in two dollars. Try to find as lucrative a retirement plan in private industry. People often forget that what they earn is more than just their salary. However, the company will tend to focus on salary as a basis for what to offer you, *unless* you take the initiative and "educate" them on the specifics of your total compensation package.

There is a distinct line between manipulating the facts of your salary history in your own best interest and outright lying. If for no other reason than it's easy to get caught lying, you should focus on the more subtle process of not overlooking any important components of your compensation and presenting the information in a manner that places you in the most favorable light.

Overcoming Common Salary Objections

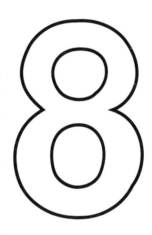

The path to a successful salary negotiation depends on your ability to overcome the inevitable objections that will be raised. While it's impossible to completely prepare for every objection you might hear, there are a few that come up time and time again:

> We don't have that much money budgeted for this position.

> You weren't earning anywhere close to that amount in your past job.

> We have employees with background similar to yours who don't make that much money.

Let's discuss how to handle each of these common stumbling blocks to successful negotiating.

Budgetary Constraints   **We don't have that much money budgeted for the position.**   Remember, most companies establish a salary range for their positions. The "top dollar" that is quoted by the employer is typically the midpoint in the range. Normally the employer can go up another 20 percent and not exceed the salary range. However, the employer's willingness to go above the midpoint depends on your ability to convince the interviewer you have the skills the employer needs. The more you can demonstrate the value you bring to the organization, the more flexible the employer will become.

It may be true that the employer hasn't budgeted for a salary above the midpoint. However, that is not the same thing as being unable to pay above the midpoint. Department heads are accountable for their total budget, not each individual line item. The individual items are helpful in establishing the total budget, not the other way around. Thus, if a manager overspends on salaries, the deficit can usually be made up by cutting or deferring expenses in some other category.

It's also important to remember that the dollars you're discussing are relatively small when compared to the total department budget. Six or eight thousand dollars may represent a large sum of money to us. For most companies, however, it is little more than a rounding error.

Finally, hiring top-quality people is one of the most important functions of management. If the company doesn't have the right people in the right jobs at the right time, the company's ability to remain competitive in challenging economic times is reduced. Thus, managers can easily justify paying more than they had budgeted in order to attract a top-quality individual. Your challenge is to convince management that you are worth the extra money. If you can establish your expertise, knowledge, and potential value to the new company, the objection of money budgeted quickly fades away.

Your Salary History   **You weren't earning anywhere close to that amount in your past job.**   This objection is designed to challenge your self-worth and can have devastating effects. Employers find this objection to be particularly effective.

Overcoming this objection requires that you focus on the value you bring to the job, rather than how much, or little, you have earned in the past. You are not seeking a merit increase; rather, you are discussing how your background and experience can help the employer accomplish a specific task. You expect to be paid for the quality of the work you perform. The fact that you were paid less in your previous position should be a non-issue as far as you are concerned. What is relevant at this point in the discussion is how you can help the company achieve its objectives. Your argument to the company is that you have the necessary skills to do the job. Your skills are what the company should be basing its salary offer. If you fit the background you should expect to be paid as much as any other individual they would hire for the job. Your market value should be determined by the value you bring to the job, not on what you earned in the past.

This objection can also be countered by the results of your research into what similar position pay in the industry. Don't be afraid of quoting this research if the offer is unrealistically low and represents only a nominal increase over your past earnings.

Management Views on Employee Equity

We have employees with similar backgrounds who don't earn that much money. This third objection is another non-issue, from your perspective. What the company pays its other workers could hardly be of less concern to you. The focus of the conversation should be on the value *you* bring to the company, not how much other people make. How the pay practices of the company affect other workers isn't your concern.

Make sure you overcome each of these objections from an attitude of self-confidence. Don't let these objections make you feel uncertainty about your market value. Don't be afraid to go on the offensive and challenge the company. Exactly how are people rewarded in the organization? Does the company recognize an individual's value and personal achievements, or does everyone receive the same increase each year? Doesn't the company financially reward those who make the greatest contribution? Often the best defense is a good offense. No company wants to be viewed as similar to the government, where everyone receives the same raise regardless of the value they contribute to the group. Companies wish to be perceived as organizations that pay for performance and recognize individual achievements through their compensation programs. Don't be afraid of challenging the company on these issues. You are likely to find that these obstacles quickly crumble.

Misconceptions About Salary Negotiating

Since little information is available about salary negotiating, it is a topic fraught with lore and legend. In the absence of facts, myths about the process that have sprung up are now accepted as gospel.

Misconceptions Revealed

Many of these misconceptions are self-limiting. We say to ourselves, "Since I don't know much about negotiating and I'm uncomfortable with what little I do know, I'll seek out any reason I can to justify not negotiating." Job changers take solace in these myths and as a result never earn the type of salary they potentially could earn. They proceed through their career certain that they are being underpaid, yet at a loss for what to do about it.

As you begin to hone your salary negotiating skills, you

will meet many people who accept these misconceptions as
fact. They use them as an excuse to not negotiate aggressively and will attempt to convince you that your efforts at
salary negotiating are pure folly. If you don't know the
truth behind the myths, you, too, may become resigned to
the belief that attempts at salary negotiation are not worth
the effort. If you understand the realities of the situation,
however, you will be able to take the nay-sayers with the
proverbial grain of salt and proceed along your course.

Let's examine some of the more common misconceptions
associated with salary negotiating.

MISCONCEPTION: At large companies salaries are prede-
termined by corporate policy so there is no point in trying
to negotiate.

REALITY: Most companies establish salary ranges for
each position in their company. The process is often quite
complex, but it ensures that individuals holding similar
jobs in the organization are compensated in an equitable
manner. Salary ranges also ensure that the position is
competitive with similar positions in the community.

The key to negotiating with larger companies is to understand and keep in mind that these companies evaluate
jobs in terms of salary ranges, not in specific dollar figures.
The range for a particular job can be quite broad.

Ranges are established to provide a minimum salary, a
midpoint figure, and the maximum salary one can earn in
the position. If you have little or no experience to bring to
the job, you would expect to be paid somewhere between
the minimum and the midpoint of the range.

The salary assigned to the midpoint is generally considered to be the wage paid to a "fully functioning professional"; in other words, someone who can come in and hit
the ground running. Salaries between the midpoint and
the maximum represent increasing amounts of experience.

Most companies try to hire someone between the minimum and the midpoint. When the company says the top
dollar they can pay is $35,000, they are usually referring
to the midpoint figure. Thus the company may actually
have considerably more discretion in offering a higher salary to the right person. The trick is that you have to convince them that you have the skills necessary to qualify for
a higher salary. We'll discuss how to do this in another
chapter.

It's also important for you to keep in mind that the salary range for a particular job can be quite large. The
spread between the minimum and the midpoint is typically

20 percent. For example, a job that has a $40,000 midpoint would have a minimum salary of $32,000 and a maximum of $48,000. It is apparent that the company often has more dollars to negotiate with than they would like you to realize. Knowing how salary ranges work can help you in the negotiating process.

Finally, keep in mind that many larger corporations allow their employees to know what the salary range is for their job. While an employee usually isn't allowed to know the ranges of the jobs above him or her, that employee's own salary range is often communicated quite openly. It is not inappropriate for you to ask what the salary range is for the position you're applying for. If you go on to ask what the position's midpoint is, you will establish yourself as a savvy negotiator who knows how the game is played.

MISCONCEPTION: All salaries are negotiable.

REALITY: Regardless of your negotiating prowess, not all salaries are negotiable. Some companies expect you to negotiate, while others operate with a "take it or leave it" attitude. The key is to know when it's appropriate to negotiate without alienating your potential employer.

Don't negotiate salary just for the sake of negotiating. Successful negotiation depends first on your fully understanding the components of the total compensation package and what your skills are worth on the market. If you have these two pieces of information and you are offered a competitive package, don't feel compelled to negotiate just for the thrill of it. You're far more likely to alienate your future boss than you are to extract more benefits and perks. Salary negotiating is about picking up all of the money the company puts on the table. It's not about squeezing a company for every last dime.

You must also pay attention to the realities of the job market. Certain industries are more open to negotiating salary than others. On one end of the scale is the government where you are paid based on a precise formula. Vacations and other benefits are also set in stone. Although you may not be able to negotiate with the government on your compensation, you can take solace in the fact that everyone else at your level is being paid approximately the same. Promotions are largely determined through a precise formula based largely on seniority. While there is a certain amount of security gained by working for the government (although no job is guaranteed), it is probably not an environment that an active negotiator will enjoy working in.

On the other end of the scale are smaller fast-growth companies. These organizations need people who can be immediately productive. Smaller companies often do not have established pay scales and often will pay what it takes to attract the right person. Obviously these companies are looking for the seasoned veteran rather than the recent college graduate who is long on potential but short on actual experience.

As a general rule, you'll find more room to negotiate the smaller the company you work for and the more experience you have. A freshly graduated college student going to work for a large accounting firm will have little room to negotiate. The experienced engineer actively recruited by a Silicon Valley high-tech start-up company will have lots of room to maneuver. However it's important that he or she knows what to ask for.

MISCONCEPTION: There are a lot of things more important than money in life.

REALITY: This misconception is one of those statements that is true but not accurate. No one doubts that making money by itself is not the primary source of happiness for most people. Without money, however, you may not be able to pursue the activities that provide you with those major amounts of happiness. Not being able to send your children to school, lacking the money to buy a new car, or continually worrying about how you are going to pay the bills can take the joy out of life. So while it's true that money won't buy you happiness, the absence of money isn't going to make you any more content.

Salaries are more than just the income we live on. For the majority of people, earning power is one of the primary methods by which we keep score. Our salaries tell us how we are doing both as individuals and compared to our peers. Our salaries can be a source of pride or embarrassment.

If you elected to pursue a noble though low-paying career such as teaching, it would be unreasonable to expect a six-figure income. However, if your salary is $10,000 above the average teacher's, you would justifiably take pride in how well you were doing. If your salary is $10,000 below the average, you would have concerns. Assuming job performance is not the issue, the difference in salaries arises because one teacher negotiates better than the other. Some teachers may be more adept at receiving credit for accomplishments and achievements and impressing school administrators with the value they bring to the organization. These are key components of salary negotiating, which we will explore in greater detail in a later chapter.

MISCONCEPTION: I don't believe in negotiating since my work will speak for itself.

REALITY: Ah, if only it were true. Many people shy away negotiating because they erroneously believe that the company will look after them and recognize their good work. They believe that producing good work is all they have to do to ensure that they are paid at the top of the scale. Unfortunately, the company does not necessarily reward the person who does the best work. The company rewards the person they *perceive* as doing the best work. These persons are not always the same. Yes, you must perform good work in order to maximize your earings. If you expect to be rewarded, however, you have to make sure the company knows about your accomplishments. You can't sit back and expect that the company will automatically appreciate your efforts.

This type of passive approach to your career can spell disaster. If we have learned any lesson from the countless numbers of reorganizations and layoffs that have swept through virtually every industry in America, it is that each person is ultimately responsible for his or her own career. Corporations are not in business to provide you with a raise or even a guarantee of continued employment. They are in business to manufacture a product, deliver a service, and make a profit. You are only employed to help the company achieve this primary task. The company doesn't owe you a job. You owe yourself a job.

People who assume the company will take care of them when it comes time for increases and promotions also assume that the company is paying attention to their efforts. Unfortunately, this is often not the case. Your good works may get lost in the shuffle or become blurred and indistinguishable from the good works of all your fellow workers. Thus, you have to take the initiative to be an aggressive spokesperson for your own self interests. The person who cares most about your career, your raise, your promotion, has to be you. If you delegate this responsibility to your employer, you are giving up control over your career.

You need to chronicle your accomplishments and achievements over the course of each year. The perception your employer has about you at raise time is largely determined by your reminding your boss of your accomplishments during the year. Don't take a passive approach to your career. If you stay active and involved, you will feel better about your job and more in control of your life.

MISCONCEPTION: I can improve my odds of getting a job by offering to work for less money.

REALITY: It's surprising how many people believe this to be true. Hiring an employee is not like buying a car. Employers do not look for the cheapest person they can find to fill an opening. They look for the most capable individual they can find.

Offering your services at a discount reflects negatively on you. Employers are surprised when you place less than market value on your skills. They may want to reevaluate why they thought you were a good candidate in the first place. Most companies believe in the old saying "You get what you pay for." Although your intentions may be good, by offering to accept a lower salary, you will cheapen yourself in the eyes of the employer.

MISCONCEPTION: Once I have established my value to the company, my salary will increase and I will be in a stronger position to negotiate.

REALITY: The most important negotiation you have with an employer is your initial starting salary. The reason this salary is so important is that all future raises and promotions will be based on a percentage of this amount. Your future earning power will be largely determined by the salary you negotiated coming in the door.

While it is true that your salary is likely to increase as you prove yourself within the organization, you may be disappointed by the rate at which it increases. Raises are given in percentages and have been running at an average of 4–6 percent in recent years. This trend is likely to continue in the future. If you receive a raise of 7–8 percent, you should consider yourself very fortunate. Although you may be successful in convincing your boss that you deserve a larger increase, it's doubtful that any further increase will add up to more than an additional 1–2 percent, and the increase will still be based on your existing base salary. This is the reason why negotiating on the front end is so important.

Some people think that the way out of the trap is through promotions. It's certainly true that a promotional raise will be bigger than a annual merit increase. However, most companies are reluctant to raise an individual's compensation dramatically in one jump. Most promotions amount to an increase of 15–18 percent over your former salary. That's a nice increase, but hardly enough for you to adopt a new standard of living. Although you can certainly improve your fortunes through promotions, your starting salary will be a major factor in how much you will earn for many years to come.

The Salary Review Meeting

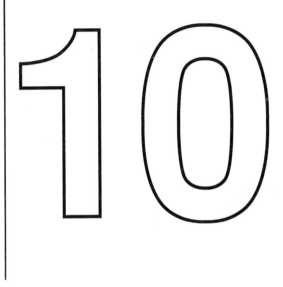

Unfortunately, your company probably isn't going to give you a large salary increase just because they want you to feel good. If that were the case, there would be little need for you to develop salary negotiating skills. Companies will base your increase largely on your perceived value to the organization. Ironically, your increase will be determined in part by how afraid the company is that you might leave. Although anyone can be replaced, the more you have carved out a niche for yourself, the more you will tend to be rewarded. In order to receive the maximum increase possible, you have to make sure that your boss fully appreciates your achievements over the past year.

Proving Your Value

Some individuals during their salary review successfully argue that they are underpaid compared to co-workers performing a similar job. While you should be aggressive in correcting this inequity, this strategy will only work once or twice. Besides, if you are an effective salary negotiator, you should never be at the bottom of the pay scale.

Companies will determine your increase based on your contribution. Unfortunately, the process for assessing and remembering your contributions over the past year is often inadequate. This is especially true if your accomplishments don't neatly correspond to the timing of the salary review. For example, if your big accomplishment occurred in January, but you're not reviewed until July, you may discover that your achievement has been forgotten. Companies sometimes revert to the school of thinking that asks, "So what have you done for me lately?"

The key for success in the salary review discussion is preparation. You need to be familiar with salary ranges and ranges for salary increases in your field. Most importantly, you need to review all of your accomplishments during the past year.

This last step is often overlooked, with dire consequences. Many people go into the salary review discussion assuming that management will remember their contribution. As we noted earlier, management's memory is notoriously short term. The responsibility is on your shoulders to ensure that you get the credit you deserve.

Identify Your Accomplishments

The first step is to sit down and review all of your activities for the past year. Think about the projects you worked on, the specific role you played, and the results achieved. The more you can quantify your results, the better. However, don't get discouraged if your projects were only a small piece of a larger company initiative. Your role was still important.

Identifying your accomplishments is difficult. This is especially true if you haven't thought about your achievements in a long while. Although the process may not be easy, it is well worth the effort. Use the following worksheet to jog your memory. Write out as many examples as you can. At this stage in the process, don't worry about wording or writing style. What's important is to begin the process of recalling your activities over the past year.

What have you . . .

Created?

_____

_____

_____

_____

Organized?

_____

_____

_____

_____

Established?

_____

_____

_____

_____

Initiated?

_____

_____

_____

_____

Revamped?

_____

_____

_____

_____

Developed?

_____

_____

_____

_____

Supervised?

_____

_____

_____

_____

Streamlined?

_____

_____

_____

_____

Strengthened?

_____

_____

_____

_____

Put into Effect?

_____

_____

_____

_____

Designed?

_____

_____

_____

_____

Reduced?

_____

_____

_____

_____

Saved?

_____

_____

_____

_____

Improved?

_____

_____

_____

_____

Increased?

_____

_____

_____

_____

Trained?

_____

_____

_____

_____

Obtain a Performance Review Form

The second step is to obtain a performance review form. Look at the criteria on which you will be evaluated. They may include such characteristics as initiative, time management, attention to detail, or communication skills. These are the criteria your company has stated are important for success. Since management will be evaluating you on these criteria, they will be more likely to reward you if you can demonstrate strengths in these areas.

Now go back to your list of accomplishments. Which of your achievements best demonstrates the traits on the evaluation form? When have you demonstrated initiative? Time management? Your ability to communicate effectively? Expand each accomplishment and focus on how you demonstrated these skills.

Putting our accomplishments down on paper is sometimes difficult. A tool many people use to help themselves is to remember the letters **S A R**.

First, write down the Situation you faced. For example: "The department was not as efficient as it could be because it did not have an inventory control system in place."

Second, write down the Action you took. "I researched what type of inventory control systems other companies our size had and made a recommendation on the most cost-effective system to senior management."

Finally, write down the Result you achieved. "My recommendation was approved by senior management and was implemented over the next 90 days. As a result, we were able to better track product costs and the efficiency of the department was increased."

What types of traits do we associate with the person who achieved this accomplishment? Initiative? Time management? By articulating your accomplishments in this manner you will remind management of the role you have played. You will have demonstrated how your strengths match up with the skills the company thinks are important.

Communicate the Information Beforehand

Now that you have completed your homework, you have to present this information to your boss in the way that will do you the most good. If you wait until the day of your review, it will probably be too late. Your salary increase will already have been decided. Remember, the salary review meeting is a time in which information is communicated, not negotiated. In order for you to benefit, your boss must receive this information well in advance of the meeting. Once the decision on your increase has been made, it will be very difficult to change management's mind.

The best way to communicate your accomplishments over the past year is through a memo. Write to your boss approximately one month in advance. Be forthright about the purpose of the memo. For example:

> As you are aware, April 15th is my annual salary review date. Like all employees, I take this process seriously and appreciate the effort you will be making to objectively access my performance. To assist you in that regard, I have prepared a brief outline of what I consider to be my major accomplishments over the past year. I look forward to discussing this further with you on the 15th.

It would be very difficult now for any boss to not give you adequate credit for the work you have performed. In fact, in the face of such concrete data, it would be difficult for most bosses not to reward you with the highest possible raise.

It is surprising that more employees don't invest the time necessary to ensure that they receive the maximum raise possible. Relying on our boss to remember our accomplishments takes us out of the driver's seat. The key for success in every aspect of salary negotiating is to maintain control. So remember: Invest some time in reviewing your accomplishments over the past year. Highlight the accomplishments which most closely match your company's performance criteria. Communicate this by memo to your boss at least one month in advance of the review meeting. These steps will help you to ensure that you are getting every dollar you have coming to you.

Handling Stressful Situations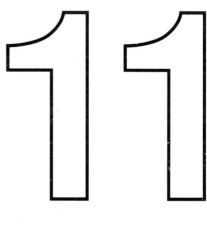

The negotiating process can be very stressful. You desperately want to win, yet you don't know how important winning is to the other party. What will they be willing to give up? Where will they draw the line? How can you best articulate your point of view? It's natural that you would feel nervous before an important negotiation.

Part of the stress you may feel is due to pent-up emotions and adrenaline. You've thought long and hard about what you're going to say and how you're going to say it. Now comes the payoff. Even the most seasoned negotiators may feel a sea of emotional turmoil beneath their calm exteriors. The only negotiators not likely to feel stress are those who don't particularly care about the outcome. When the subject is salaries, however, no one takes a "don't care" attitude.

While internal stress is a challenge, intentional external stress can wreak havoc with your salary negotiating plans. Intentional external stress is caused by specific activities initiated by the other party with whom you are negotiating. While these tactics may not be outright dirty tricks, they are designed to keep you off-balance and give your opponent an advantage. The key to handling these stressful situations is to maintain your composure and a level head. If you use common sense and don't lose your equilibrium, you won't let these tactics throw you.

Let's look at some of the more common ploys.

Sun in Your Eyes   You enter the room and are motioned to a seat in front of the desk. The sun streams in from the window—directly into your face. You begin to feel your temperature rise and sweat breaking out on your forehead. Your collar starts to feel uncomfortably tight. It becomes difficult to look your opponent in the eye. His face gradually becomes an orange ball. Your carefully prepared opening statement gets lost in your stress.

It is surprising that this method is as effective as it is, since the solution is so obvious. Despite the easy solution, many people respond to this ploy like sheep being led off to slaughter. They sit where they are told to sit, regardless of how uncomfortable the arrangement. One could say that people this easily manipulated deserve the paltry salary they can "negotiate."

The key to avoiding this trap is awareness and self-confidence. Just because a chair is offered to you doesn't mean you have to sit in it. When you enter the office, make sure you take in the surroundings. Look at the furniture and where it's located. Observe your overall surroundings. Look at the chair that is offered to you. If sunlight is hitting it, simply move it to a place where it is out of the glare. Don't even ask permission. Assume that no one would want you to sit in the sun. If the sun completely covers the desk, call the person's bluff. "How about if we move over here to get out of the sun?" Once you draw attention to the ploy, your opponent will never force you to sit in such an uncomfortable spot. This intentionally stressful situation can be easily handled if you keep your presence of mind.

One Leg Is Short on the Chair   This ploy is a variation on the "sun in your eyes" gambit. The solution is easy and obvious. By drawing attention to the wobbly chair, you will unmask the obvious attempt at putting you in an uncomfortable position. You'll score points for your side by saying, "There seems to be something wrong with this chair. Would you mind if I used this one?"

A Multiple Audience

Sometimes during the interview process the salary negotiations are left to the very end, and you may be brought back one more time to work out the final details. Upon arriving, you discover that you are not dealing one-on-one, but rather with a group of people. The audience may consist of your future boss, his boss, the recruiter from personnel, and the compensation manager. This can be intimidating if you've never dealt with groups before.

First, the good news. The advantage of having everyone in the room is that any questions can be quickly resolved. All the experts and decision makers are present. Negotiations won't have to be delayed because the interviewer needs to check with personnel to see if an exception to a policy can be made.

The disadvantage of this situation is that each of the experts can now pick on you individually. Their goal will be to tell you that as much as they would like to meet your salary needs, they think that the fairest arrangement would be to reward you once you've proven yourself on the job. Since they take turns coming at you, it's difficult to focus your attention and easy to find yourself distracted. Even though you know what you should say, articulating it to a group is different than selling your proposal one-on-one.

One problem you may encounter is that addressing a group of people can throw off your timing. Knowing who to concentrate on is very important. One of the important strategies to effectively negotiating with a group is the proper use of eye contact.

When you are asked a question by one member of the group, start your answer by looking that person in the eye. As you continue your answer shift your glance to look at everyone else individually. By the time you have finished answering the question, you should have looked each person in the eye at least once. Try to finish your answer by looking at the person who originally asked the question.

The advantage of this method is twofold. First, you will cut down on interruptions. Second, by looking at everyone as you give your answer, you will be more effective in convincing the group. Remember, you can't sell someone unless you look them in the eye. Make a conscious effort to shift your eye contact as you talk. "I appreciate your position and agree that my long-term compensation should be tied to performance. However, as we are both aware, these increases will be based on a percentage of my starting salary. The starting salary I'm asking for is fair and competitive."

✓ *Coffee*

It might be hard to believe, but the goodwill gesture of a cup of coffee can be used by your opponent as an effective tool against you. You should think twice before accepting.

Remember that you're bound to be a little nervous in the meeting. When you're nervous a faint tremor may occur in your hand. Since hot coffee tends to spill very easily, you may find that all of the coffee has not remained in the cup. If it spills on your hand, or drips onto your slacks, how effective do you think you will be in remembering the points you wanted to make about the bonus plan?

You have the cup of coffee and you've taken your first sip. Now it's time to put the cup down . . . where? Perhaps on the nice Chippendale desk corner where it will leave a ring. Maybe you can balance it precariously on a stack of newspapers. Or maybe you'll just keep holding onto it, hoping that the slight tremor doesn't come back into your hand. Who's got the upper hand in the negotiations now?

Although most negotiators will play a fair game with you, everyone is looking to gain an edge in the process. If someone can affect the physical surroundings to give themselves an advantage, they'll probably do so. This doesn't mean that you should become paranoid about the motivation behind every gesture. Few negotiators manage their physical space as did the late Harry Cohen.

For over twenty years Harry Cohen was the boss and monarch of Columbia Pictures. He lived to negotiate and used every advantage he could to achieve his goals. His office personified an environment designed to intimidate all but the most confident of talent.

The office was rectangular, with the door on one end and Cohen's desk on the other. The desk was raised three feet off the ground so that the visitor was always looking up at Cohen. Although Cohen himself was a small man, he overcame this liability through the design of his office. While you are unlikely to encounter anything this extreme, remember that the purpose of the meeting is to negotiate your salary. Everything else either helps or hinders you in achieving this objective. Don't be distracted. Don't lose your self-confidence. If you find that you are suddenly uncomfortable, remember that it may be by design. Don't let intentional external forces throw you from your preparation.

What Kind of Salary Do You Want?

Perhaps no other interview question causes as much anxiety as this one "So, tell me, what kind of salary are you looking for?"

What are you supposed to say? Should you quote a precise figure? Talk in broad ranges? Plead indifference? Respond humorously? What exactly are you worth?

Not knowing your market value is a huge obstacle in the salary negotiation process. The results of not knowing what you are worth can be disastrous. If you ask for $30,000, but the employer was willing to go to $35,000, it's unlikely that they will pay you the extra five thousand dollars simply out of the goodness of their hearts.

Broaching the Subject Ideally, the subject of salaries will be deferred to the end of the interview. Ideally, but not realistically. The question may be the first one out of the interviewer's mouth, or the last. Or it may come up somewhere in the middle. Although there is no way to predict when the subject of salaries will be raised, you can rest assured that it will come up. You must be prepared.

Sometimes the salary issue first comes up when you're filling out the employment application. While most of us hate filling out these forms, they are a necessary evil. This is especially true if you are applying for an entry-level position. The good news is that as you progress through the management ranks, the use of employment applications drops considerably. In many companies, middle managers are only asked to fill out the application as a formality. In fact, many middle managers fill out the form only after they have been hired. Executives recruited for senior-level spots never fill out applications. However, if you are in the early stages of your career, resign yourself to the inevitability of applications and fill them out with as much good humor as you can.

The Application

The salary question on an employment application is the employer's first attempt to get you to name your price. As much as the employer would like for you to tip your hand, doing so is not in your best interest. Write "negotiable," "open," or "will discuss." Most companies won't press you at this point to specify the dollar amount you're looking for.

As in any negotiation, you're better off by having the discussion about money occur later rater than earlier. This allows you a greater opportunity to impress the company with your background and potential. Naturally, the company views this issue in exactly the opposite manner. They want to know about your salary requirements as early as possible so that they can quickly rule you in or out as a candidate. It's important that you realize this fundamental difference between your objectives and theirs if you are going to navigate this sensitive area successfully.

Revealing Salary Requirements

For example, newspaper help-wanted ads commonly request that candidates "state their salary requirements." Some ads even go on to say "No applications will be considered without salary information." Such statements are little more than hogwash. No company in its right mind is going to rule you out solely because you did not include how much money you expect to make. If it did, it is probably not the type of company you would want to work for anyway. By not including this information, you are just making the employment department's job a little more difficult. While you do not want to needlessly annoy anyone in the hiring process, you're better off by not committing yourself to a salary number this early in the game.

It's an entirely different issue when this question comes up in the interview. How you handle this question will not only impact the amount of money you will be offered, but also influences how the company views you as a candidate.

The Money or the Job!

Keep in mind that the money question has two different agendas. Yes, the company wants to know how much you expect to make, but it also wants to determine which is more important to you—the money or the job? If you emphasize money and ramble on about how you haven't been fairly compensated in the past, you'll come across as a greedy complainer. If you go the opposite direction and leave the impression that money doesn't matter to you one bit, you'll come across as a fool. Your answer should strike a balance. You want to position yourself as being primarily interested in the opportunity but expecting to be paid a very competitive wage.

A good way to answer this question is to begin as follows: "Well, Mr. Employer, like everyone else, I want to make as much money as I can; however, I'm mostly excited about the challenges involved in the assignment. From what you've told me, it seems that my background matches up well with what needs to be done."

Tactics

At this stage you can try to turn the tables on the interviewer by persuading him or her to articulate how much the company is willing to pay: "Let me ask you, what kind of money do you have budgeted for this position?"

The key word here is "budgeted." Even though salaries are a subject we feel passionately about, they are, after all, simply a line-item budget figure. Referring to your potential salary as a budgeted chunk of money, not dissimilar to office supplies, can sometimes cause the interviewer to tip his or her hand: "Well, we were thinking of bringing someone in between $45,000 and $50,000."

A moment ago you may have been perfectly happy with $45,000. Now you realize that there is more money on the table than you originally thought. You can maximize your position by bracketing the higher end of the quoted figure: "That would seem fair; I've been exploring opportunities in the $49,000 to $54,000 range."

This tactic tends to work better on line managers than it does on human resource department recruiters. The line managers typically have less experience interviewing than personnel and often tend to think in terms of budgeted numbers.

While this tactic is worth trying, don't be surprised if your request for budgeted salary information is politely deflected. Interviewers usually won't take offense at your attempt. In fact they'll often give you credit for making the attempt. Many interviewers will deflect your query with a statement such as, "I'm not sure. It will depend on the individual. So tell me, what type of money are you looking for?"

Ultimately, you must be prepared to discuss salaries. Based on the research you've conducted, mention a salary range, not a specific number. By speaking in terms of ranges, you are less likely to leave money on the table inadvertently.

Make sure your range is reasonable. Saying that you're looking at opportunities that pay from $35,000 to $80,000 will only make you look silly. Refusing to state a range makes you appear obstinate. Neither impression is helpful if you want to receive an offer.

A range of $5,000 is appropriate for people starting out their careers and $10,000–$15,000 for mid-level employees. Quite broad ranges are appropriate for extremely seasoned executives. The following are examples of how you might describe your range.

> I'm seriously considering opportunities in the range of $27,000 to $32,000.

> My expectations are from the mid-thirties to the mid to high forties.

> My total compensation, which includes base salary, bonus, stock, and longer term incentives, was in the mid–six figures. I would expect your financial package to provide adequate incentives.

The higher one goes in the organization, the more obliquely specific dollar amounts are referred to. In the early stages of your career, however, it's important that you know your specific worth so you can handle the question of money to your best advantage.

Executive Recruiters | 13

Executive recruiters or headhunters, as they are commonly referred to, are a misunderstood group. The role they play in the employment process is often considerable. Although recruiters participate in filling less than 20 percent of job openings, they have a lot of clout. In many instances they are trusted and highly valued advisors to senior management.

Recruiters can be helpful in a number of ways. They can help you identify opportunities, give you more information about salaries in your field, and assist you in the negotiation process. It's worthwhile to learn about how they operate.

Recruiting Professionals

The executive recruiting profession is a relatively young industry that has grown considerably in stature over the past ten years. Its origins trace back to the 1960s when many of the leading executive recruiting firms were established. The recruiting business originally began as a component of the services provided by the large general management consulting and Big Eight accounting firms. As the recruiting business grew, the consulting and accounting firms recognized a potential conflict of interest between their recruiting work and the other services they provided to other clients. The accounting profession in particular came under criticism for recruiting chief financial officers who would then be responsible for determining which accounting firm conducted the company's annual audit.

By the late 1960s, many firms had spun off their recruiting practices, which accelerated the growth of the industry. Early pioneers such as Korn Ferry, Russell Reynolds, Heidrick & Struggles, and Spencer Stuart grew into major players. They in turn spun off new competition. Today the executive search industry consists of two tiers of firms: large multinational organizations and smaller boutique firms. The latter tends to specialize in a particular industry or function while the former has the capability to quickly implement an international search.

Much of the confusion associated with recruiting firms is due to a misunderstanding about how they operate. Regardless of their size, recruiting firms represent companies, not individuals. Companies hire recruiting firms to assist them in finding candidates for a particular opening. Individuals don't hire recruiting firms to find them a job.

This misunderstanding accounts for much of the disgruntlement sometimes felt toward recruiting firms. Statements such as "They didn't seem very interested in me," or "The recruiter didn't do anything for me" are common. Both of these statements reflect that the individuals didn't understand who the recruiter represents.

Recruiters will be most interested in meeting you if they have a position that matches your background. If they're not working on an appropriate search, you realistically can't expect them to spend a great deal of time with you. Although a recruiter may not be working on a search in your field, most recruiters are interested in meeting new people who may in the future develop into future clients or candidates. However, you must be sensitive to the demands you place on the recruiter's time. If you're seeking to establish a relationship with a particular recruiter, be willing to meet them early in the morning or after normal business hours. Flexibility on your part can go a long way toward establishing the relationship.

A Specialized Industry

The recruiting industry has become increasingly specialized. Recruiters usually focus on a particular function, industry, or on positions paying certain amounts of money. Since most of the work is done over the phone, recruiters are not limited to performing searches only in their own locale.

There are two kinds of recruiting firms: *contingency* and *retained*. The difference between the two pertains to how each is paid and the types of positions each works on. Fees are paid to both kinds of firms by the client company and not the individual. Let's take a look at how each of these firms works and the differences between them.

Contingency Recruiting Firms

Contingency firms generally work on assignments paying $50,000 or less. They earn their fee only if the company actually hires a person referred by the agency. Thus, their fee is contingent upon the company actually hiring their candidate. If the company hires someone from an ad in the paper, from a competing contingency firm, or from walking in off the street, the agency doesn't make a dime.

This form of fee structure has its critics, and some contingency firms have been charged with unscrupulous behavior. Since the company is not on the hook for a fee unless someone from the contingency firm is hired, companies typically will give out the recruiting assignment to a number of contingency firms. Often the company will also run help-wanted ads in the paper. This can set off a mad scramble among the contingency firms to see who can submit candidates the quickest to the employer. Less than completely ethical agencies have been known to "float" resumes to employers in the hope that something will stick. Thus it's possible that your resume might be sent to companies without your knowledge. This can cheapen your image and hurt your chances of negotiating the best possible compensaton package.

As in any field, there are good and poor players in the recruiting industry. Good recruiters can help plan your salary negotiating strategy and assist you in getting top dollar. Poor recruiters can undermine the process and cause great harm.

Fortunately, there is a rather simple strategy to identify and screen the best contingency recruiters in your field. First, your goal should be to work with only a handful of the best firms. Three to five firms who specialize in either your industry or function is an optimal number.

Since companies typically give out contingency assignments to multiple agencies, you want to make sure that your resume isn't being indiscriminately mailed all over town. This cheapens your image and looks unprofessional.

You can identify which firms specialize in your field through the *Directory of Executive Recruiters* published by Kennedy & Kennedy in Fitzwilliam, New Hampshire. This directory is acknowledged as the bible of the industry, and the editors are very careful to ensure that the information listed about recruiting firms is accurate. The book identifies firms by function, industry, and location. Don't worry much about location, since most recruiters have clients nationwide. Since the bulk of recruiting work is done over the phone, where the recruiter actually lives reflects primarily personal preference.

Develop your initial list of recruiters and then proceed to interview them over the telephone. Contingency recruiters tend to be easier to reach on the telephone than retained recruiters who work the upper end of the market. Ask if the recruiter specializes in your field and how long they have been in the recruiting business. Contingency recruiters are paid on commission, and there is a high rate of turnover among recruiters.

Although there is no licensing process for recruiters, look for individuals who have earned the Certified Personnel Consultant designation. This means they have been in the recruiting business for a minimum of two years and have passed an examination. Although there are many good recruiters who are not CPCs, this certification is one indication of competency.

Retained Recruiting Firms

The second type of recruiter is the *retained recruiter*. These recruiters work to fill jobs that generally pay a minimum of $50,000 to $75,000. Many retained recruiters do not work on assignments that pay less than $100,000. The retained recruiters are paid their fee regardless of whether they complete the assignment. They receive their fee even if the company hires a candidate from another source. The retained recruiters liken themselves to the doctor or lawyer who gets paid even if the case is lost or the patient doesn't improve. Kennedy's *Directory of Executive Recruiters* can also help you identify the retained recruiting firms which work in your field. If your market value has not yet reached $50,000, however, you are better off focusing on contingency firms.

Establishing a relationship with a contingency or retained recruiter is a savvy career move. Since these people keep their finger on the pulse of the marketplace, they are an invaluable source on job leads and trends in compensation. They can be particularly helpful to senior level managers by keeping them informed of new trends in compensation. This is important when you receive your income from a variety of sources including short- and long-term bonus plans. A recruiter can keep you abreast of how you are doing financially compared to your peers, in addition to helping you in the negotiating process.

The most effective way to work with recruiters is to establish the relationship well before you need their services. The easiest way to do this is to return the recruiter's call when they are trolling for potential candidates. By referring the recruiter to colleagues or associates, you can begin to develop a mutually beneficial relationship.

Geographic Differences 14

Salaries are not all the same. The guy down the hall in college who goes on and on about the big bucks he's pulling down in New York City might be surprised at the life-style one can afford for a fraction of the cost in St. Louis.

A variety of factors determines how much your salary will buy in different cities. When you are evaluating a salary offer in a new town, make sure you take the time to find out how much of the paycheck you'll actually get to keep. Your salary is one thing. What you can actually buy with it is often a completely different matter.

Taxes, Housing, and Expenses

Taxes are a confusing subject since many of the taxes we pay aren't referred to as taxes. For example, the mandatory car emission test you're required to get each year in

Atlanta isn't officially a tax—but in reality it is. Make sure you know about city and state income taxes in order to determine exactly how much you'll be bringing home. People living in Florida and Texas, which have no state income tax, enjoy a higher standard of living on the same dollars than their counterparts in Boston or New York.

Housing is a significant factor. Companies often have difficulty recruiting people into such cities as Los Angeles, Boston, and San Francisco because the cost of housing is dramatically higher in these cities than in other areas of the country. While you can spend $1 million for a house in Chicago if you want to, you don't really have to. There are still many cities, predominantly in the midwest and the southeast, where good affordable housing begins at $100,000. Rents are usually less dramatic in range than housing prices, but the two tend to follow parallel paths. If the housing market is pricey, the rental market also tends to be high.

Staples such as gasoline vary enormously from state to state and can eat up a large chunk of your paycheck. Gasoline that costs $1 per gallon in Dallas may cost over $1.25 in Los Angeles or Miami. This can add up quickly if you have a substantial commute.

Candidates often overlook factors such as the cost of parking when they are comparing salary offers. If you rent or purchase a condominium, parking may not be included in your monthly rent or mortgage. In some major cities you'll need another $300 per month in order to have handy access to your car. You'll also want to ask your employer about parking at work. This is often negotiable, but you'll have to ask. Employer-paid parking is a great perk, since it's usually not taxed as income. If you had to pay the parking out of your own pocket, you would be paying in after-tax dollars. You can free up some cash if you can negotiate with your employer to pick up this expense.

Visit the Location

The best way to evaluate the true cost of working in a particular city is to visit for two or three days. Many employers will allow you a house hunting trip as long as you seem sincerely interested in the opportunity. A lot of people don't take full advantage of this free trip to accurately assess the expenses of living in the city.

To comparison-shop effectively, the first step is to get a copy of the city's major newspaper. Check out rental and housing prices. Call an insurance agent and find out how much your new insurance policy will cost. Call the utility company to find out what the rates are and what an average customer pays. Although the rate may be higher, your actual costs might go down. For example, rates are fairly high in southern California, but because of the temperate climate, people actually wind up using less electricity.

Since you're likely to want a social life, check out restaurant prices, the cost of movie tickets, and how much it costs to participate in the other social activities you enjoy. For example, the cost of health club memberships varies considerably from city to city.

Finally, take a trip to the local grocery store. You're likely to spend a lot of money here, so check out the prices carefully. If you enjoy a beer in the evening, make sure you investigate the price of a six-pack lest you be unpleasantly surprised when you move to a state like Georgia, where beer is quite expensive.

Salary Offer vs. Cost of Living

Armed with this information, you are now in a position to accurately compare salary offers. There are some additional resources you may also want to use. A variety of services publish cost-of-living information for cities nationwide. This data appears in a number of trade journals and other publications. If you are interested in obtaining this information ask the research librarian at your public library for a report. *National Business Employment Weekly*, published by the *Wall Street Journal*, also publishes cost-of-living data about once a month. You can find *NBEW* on newsstands or in the placement office of a local college or university. You may also want to check *Places-Rated Almanac* published by Rand-McNally.

The data in these reports can often appear to be contradictory. Although no report will list New York or Los Angeles among the nation's cheapest places to live, estimates vary widely on the actual cost of living in different cities. This is because the statisticians who prepare these reports use different items to compare costs. For example, many reports use the price of milk to determine how much it costs to live in a particular city. A good indicator, unless you don't drink milk. Thus, you should take the guides only as a rough estimate of how expensive one city is to live in compared to another. No report can tell you exactly how much you'll need to budget. The most effective method is for you to personally investigate the city.

With that caveat in mind, what follows is a comparison

chart on the cost of living in a selected number of cities. It provides an estimate of how much you will need to have the same buying power of an average $30,000 paycheck.

Average Town U.S.A.	$30,000
San Francisco	$43,700
Los Angeles	$39,500
New York	$38,000
Washington, DC	$36,500
Boston	$35,500
Philadelphia	$33,500
Detroit	$32,700
Chicago	$32,300
Houston	$28,800
Dallas	$28,700

Source: *Young Executive Magazine*, Spring 1992.

If your potential employer is located in one of the more expensive cities, will they offer you a salary adjustment to compensate? The answer to this question is that any adjustment made is usually quite modest. Don't try negotiating for an unusually large salary offer to offset the higher cost of living. You'd be wiser to negotiate specific components of your compensation where the new higher cost of living is likely to hurt your pocketbook.

Companies simply cannot pay people large sums of money just because they are located in a more expensive city. Although salaries in New York tend to be larger than those in St. Paul, the higher amounts do not offset the cost-of-living differences. Companies can't afford to pay their employees the amount of money they would need in Boston to have the same lifestyle they enjoyed in Houston.

Cost-of-living adjustments are also difficult to manage internally. This is especially true for large corporations that continually move people from state to state. If you pay someone an extra $20,000 to move from Minneapolis to San Francisco, what happens when you promote and relocate that person to Kansas City? Do you give them a $5,000 promotional increase and take back the $20,000? While employees like receiving more money, they rebel when you try to take it away. More companies are simply acknowledging that they are located in an area with a high cost of living and screen candidates for their willingness to assume the additional financial burden. Another option an increasing number of companies are electing is to move out of the traditional high-cost locations. However, it usually won't be feasible for you to hold out from responding to an offer in anticipation that the company will move to a cheaper location.

Although companies in high-cost locations may not be willing to provide you with a large increase in base salary, this doesn't mean that there's no room to negotiate. Keep in mind that companies tend to be much more open-minded toward one-time costs that wouldn't be factored into your annual salary. A solution that often keeps both parties happy is a lump-sum payment to be made once the offer is accepted.

Moving Costs

Lump-sum payments are often negotiated as a part of the relocation package. They are typically negotiated on a case-by-case basis, and you will usually have to initiate the discussion. At a minimum, you should receive one month's salary to offset the cost of moving. Renters or recent college graduates are often offered two weeks' salary. these amounts should be considered only as the starting point from which to negotiate. The relocation package should also include the physical movement of your household goods to the new location and stay of reasonable length in a hotel while you look for new housing. Two weeks to two months, depending upon seniority, is standard. Again, the length is usually open to negotiation. While the relocation allowance has been traditionally intended to cover such costs as deposits to the phone and gas company, it is increasingly being used by companies to help compensate relocated employees for the increase in living expenses.

Another method that companies are often open to is making a low-interest or forgivable loan to the relocated employee. These loans are structured so that if you are still an employee in good standing after a period of three to five years, the loan is forgiven. There is mutual benefit to this arrangement. You are provided with some additional income and your employer knows you won't arbitrarily walk off the job. These "golden handcuff" arrangements are often in everyone's interest.

Final Details

A final point you may wish to negotiate if you are moving to a new location is the sale of your old residence. The 1990s have seen a dramatic slowdown in home sales that is likely to continue in the near future, despite lowering interest rates. Paying a larger mortgage on a new home is one thing. Having to make two house payments can sink even the most solvent of households. Besides, you'll probably need the equity from your old home as a down payment on your new residence.

Ask your new employer if they contract with a third-party relocation service. If so, make sure you take advantage of this option. The third-party relocation service is likely to offer you less money for your home than if you were willing or able to keep your house on the market for a whole year. Normally, however, you will be grateful to get out from under the old house payment. Accepting their offer can free up some needed capital. Again, such arrangements are often negotiable, especially for experienced managers.

Moving to a new location requires that you first research the difference in costs. Don't rely too heavily on the published statistics, except as a rough guide. Invest the time personally to determine how expensive your new location will be to live in and then negotiate with your employer on an individual basis. You may discover that such items as parking, car allowances, and even country club membership can be negotiated in lieu of a large increase in your base salary.

Use the following chart as a guide when calculating cost of living in a new city.

COST OF LIVING ANALYSIS

Annual Cost of . . .	Current City	Prospective City
Taxes	_____	_____
Housing	_____	_____
Food	_____	_____
Transportation	_____	_____
Insurance	_____	_____
Utilities	_____	_____
Entertainment	_____	_____
Club Memberships	_____	_____

Counteroffers

One of the sure signs of job search and salary negotiating success is getting a counteroffer. Receiving a counteroffer is flattering and seductive. You are showered with reasons for why you should not leave good old XYZ Corp. The praise, to say nothing of the additional money, are powerful inducements for you to stay. However, when all the dust settles, it is usually a terrible mistake to accept a counteroffer.

Setting the Terms

Let's define our terms. Counteroffers are those inducements from your current employer to get you to stay once you have announced your intention to accept a new position. Although there may be a few individuals who have accepted a counteroffer and gone on to have a successful career, their numbers are few. For most people, a counteroffer does nothing to address the underlying issues behind the decision to seek new employment. Management recruiters and human resources executives estimate that up to 80 percent of managers accepting counteroffers subsequently leave their employer within one year.

The reason counteroffers don't work has to do with that somewhat antiquated notion of company loyalty. Although we can argue in this age of downsizings and restructurings that employee loyalty is a concept of the past, there still exists a strong sense of loyalty between supervisors and their employees. Accepting an offer from another company upsets that bond. It's not your loyalty to good old XYZ company that is being called into question, but rather your loyalty to the department. Thus the boss's reaction is quite commonly a very personal and negative one. "How could this person be doing this to me?" your boss may ask.

On the pragmatic level, a number of things happen when you announce your planned departure. Business plans are upset, work must be redistributed, vacations are postponed, and life generally becomes much more difficult for everyone in the department. It's not surprising that counteroffers are made. "Let's keep Nancy here," your co-workers say, "at least until the first quarter is over so that we can complete the Fornortnor financing." Keeping you around so that current projects can be completed is a compelling reason to offer you attractive inducements to stay. However, remember what the motivation was behind the offer. Suddenly you've changed in the company's eyes from a long-term player to a short-term issue that needs to be dealt with. Guess who won't be getting a whole lot of new critical assignments in the future? Guess who becomes extremely expendable once the Fornortnor financing is completed? It's likely that you'll only enjoy the benefits of the counteroffer for a few months while the company immediately begins to scout around for your replacement.

Truths About Counteroffers

You should carefully consider the following universal truths before succumbing to the temptations of a counteroffer.

1. If the only way you can get a raise or promotion is to threaten to quit, you're probably better off somewhere else.

2. No matter what the company says to you when they are making the counteroffer, your loyalty will always be suspect. You will no longer be viewed as a team player, and you may find yourself dropped from the inner circle of decision makers.

3. Counteroffers are usually little more than stalling devices to give your company time to find your replacement.

4. The original frustrations you had with your employer are not likely to change. Your reasons for leaving will still exist. All the counteroffer does is improve some of the superficial circumstances or provide a short-term cash compensation.

If you've decided to accept a new position and receive a counteroffer, remember the motivation behind the offer. The odds are against you if you accept. Take the counteroffer as a compliment but don't let it obscure the more fundamental reasons you decided to conduct a job search in the first place.

Bonuses and Stock Options

16

One of the more important components of your compensation plan is the bonus and stock option program. Most people find that their base salary covers monthly operating expenses and establishes a certain standard of living. However, it is very difficult to realize considerable wealth through a monthly or weekly paycheck. When we read in the business press about the millions of dollars some executives make, the payouts are usually in the form of stock options and bonuses. Thus, we need to fully understand how these two programs work so that we can integrate them into our negotiating strategy.

Bonuses   Bonuses are usually offered to employees beginning at the middle-management ranks. Employees in line functions, such as sales, tend to participate in bonus programs earlier than individuals in staff functions, such as personnel or communications.

Bonuses are typically awarded based on a combination of factors. Three common criteria are, your personal performance, your business unit's performance, and the profitability of the entire company. There are also short- and long-term bonus programs. Short-term programs generally pay out once a year. Longer-term programs can stretch out over a number of years to encourage senior management not to excessively focus on the immediate quarter's financial results. The emphasis on short-term profitability has been a major criticism of American business and management in recent years.

What can you expect to make from a bonus plan? Senior-level executives can often double or even triple their base salary through bonuses. For most people starting out, however, a typical bonus would provide an additional 10–20 percent of income.

Most bonuses are paid out either quarterly, semiannually, or annually. As you progress upward through the management ranks, it is not unusual to participate in a number of different programs that pay out at different intervals. The higher you go in the organization, the more bonus programs you get invited to participate in. Only senior management typically participates in the longer-term incentive programs. These forms of bonuses are based on how well the company performs over a number of years. Although the money is not paid out for many years, the sums can be substantial. Long-term incentives are also an effective method of ensuring that individuals in senior management do not leave the company. Embarrassingly, some companies have seen an exodus of executives occur once multi-year bonus programs have been paid.

American businesses are increasingly using bonuses as a method to link compensation with performance. Despite numerous attempts to link annual salary increases with job performance, implementing these "pay for performance" programs has proven quite difficult. Bonuses are an easier method for rewarding top performers. Thus it's important that you make sure you fully understand about all of the bonus programs you may be eligible to participate in.

You should also consider negotiating a sign-on bonus as a part of your first-year compensation. Many companies are willing to offer you a one-time cash bonus that compensates you for some of the benefits you may be leaving behind in your old job. Although sign-on bonuses are relatively common, you'll have to remember to ask for one. Few companies will offer them voluntarily.

In order to negotiate the sign-on bonus, you'll need to determine the value of benefits you may be leaving behind. Some perks are more difficult to value than others and may not be worth including in your estimate, such as the use of an executive dining room. Other items, however, such as bonuses, stock options, and supplemental retirement programs should be included. Your goal is to remain "whole" as you change employers. You want to improve, not decrease, your standard of living by changing employers. You shouldn't just walk away from benefits you've already accrued.

For example, many companies offer supplemental executive retirement plans. These are commonly known as SERPS and are typically provided to key management personnel. These programs provide greater benefits than the ordinary worker or middle manager receives. If you are in the later years of your career, negotiating to participate in a SERP program is important. Remember, the value of most pensions is based on years of experience. If you join the company near the end of your career, you may discover that your standard employee pension will be quite small. When negotiating, it is important to consider short- and long-term financial benefits. Negotiating to participate in a SERP program can provide you with the difference between your old and new pensions.

An additional point worth negotiating is to have your new company guarantee your first-year bonus. In the first six months on the new job, you'll be getting oriented and won't be able to have a great impact on the company. There is no reason why you should be financially penalized for facing this learning curve. Asking that your first year's bonus be guaranteed is becoming increasingly standard.

Stock Options

If you want to accumulate significant wealth while you work for a company, stock options will be your vehicle. Historically, stock options were only awarded to individuals who were in senior levels of the organization. This has changed considerably in recent years. More and more companies have realized that by allowing their employees to have an investment in the company, their commitment to the organization is greater. Over the past ten years stock options have been given to employees at levels farther and farther down the organization. PepsiCo recently offered stock options to every employee in the organization. Compensation consultants expect that this trend will continue.

When one reads in the business press about the large sums of money some business executives are making, the vast majority of the income is obtained through stock options. Whether you are just starting your career or are next in line for senior management, you need to understand how the process works. Fortunately, stock options are very straightforward.

When you are issued a stock option, it gives you the right to purchase a specified number of shares at a specific price. The price is usually equal to the amount at which the stock is trading on the day you receive the option. If the stock goes down in price, the options are worthless. If the stock increases in price, you can exercise the option and pocket the difference. Stock option programs normally allow you to cash in a certain number of shares over a specified number of years. Stock options are a key component of "golden handcuff" compensation programs, which have received much attention in the business press. These programs are designed to retain the services of valued executives by making it financially beneficial for them not to leave.

Both bonus plans and stock option programs can add considerable numbers of dollars to your income. The rules for who participates is often determined by a combination of company policy and individual negotiating. This is especially true in smaller companies. Thus, make sure you fully explore how these programs work and negotiate to participate sooner rather than later.

Understanding Your Benefit Package

An often misunderstood and overlooked component of the total compensation package is your benefits. Most employees participate in a benefit plan, yet few individuals really understand what is included. This confusion is often compounded by the language used to describe employee benefits. Savvy negotiators realize that it is very important to know exactly what is included because some items can be negotiated. Although benefits are often taken for granted, they are an integral part of your total compensation package. What you don't know may wind up costing you money down the road. While benefit programs vary considerably, most include three components: medical insurance, life and disability insurance, and a retirement plan.

Medical Insurance

Companies will normally provide medical coverage for all of their full-time employees. If you are working as a temporary full-time employee, you may also receive health coverage once you have worked for the company a minimum of six months. Because of the quickly rising cost of health care, coverage is usually paid by both the employer and the employee, although the employer picks up the majority of the cost. For an additional charge you can usually purchase health coverage for your spouse and unmarried children up to the age of 25.

Make sure you know when your health coverage will begin. Some companies start coverage immediately, while others have a waiting period of a month or more. If you are faced with a waiting period, be sure to purchase a temporary insurance policy to cover the time until you are covered by your new employer. Although temporary policies are expensive, they are cheap compared to the cost of incurring a serious illness without insurance.

Another area to investigate is the way preexisting conditions will be handled. Very often you may find that any health condition that existed previously will not be covered under the new policy for an initial period of 12 months. After this waiting period preexisting conditions are normally covered in the same way as any other health problem. Potentially, however, this waiting period can mean considerable out-of-pocket expense for a newly hired employee. This contingency should be investigated thoroughly prior to accepting an offer.

Many prospective employers will offer you the opportunity to choose between a number of health care providers. These will typically include Blue Cross/Blue Shield or one of the many HMOs (health maintenance organizations). While an HMO often has lower deductibles and can cost you less, you may find yourself restricted to using only those doctors approved by the HMO. If choosing your own doctor is important to you, the higher costs of the Blue Cross/Blue Shield program may be worth it.

Life and Disability Insurance

Another typical component of a benefit program is life insurance. Companies often provide a set amount of life insurance, usually around $10,000, at no charge. Additional life insurance can be purchased by the employee at very reasonable rates.

You will also want to investigate your company's policy on total disability insurance. This form of insurance provides you with income should you become totally disabled. Many policies provide you with 60 percent of your former income. Insurance of this nature provides a financial cushion should the unthinkable happen.

Retirement Plan   This is one of the more commonly misunderstood parts of a benefit plan. Common terms used to describe retirement plans such as "matching" and "vesting" are often not clearly understood.

Typically, a retirement program will work in the following way. You will have the opportunity to invest a percentage of your pay into a retirement fund which your employer will match at a certain percentage rate. As an example, for every dollar you contribute to the fund your employer kicks in fifty cents. This sum of money can add up considerably over the years.

The term "vesting" refers to how long you have to wait before you can get the money put in by your employer should you decide to leave. In some cases you may be vested on your first day of employment, in other cases you may have to wait up to five years.

There are many other components that make up a company's benefit program. These will vary considerably from one organization to another. For example, you will want to determine which holidays your employer observes. Although there are a certain number of holidays that are observed by virtually all employers, you may wish to negotiate the right to observe dates that are of specific importance to you. A number of companies have begun the practice of allowing employees a set number of "floating" days that allow individuals to celebrate holidays of personal importance.

The length of vacation is typically determined by how long one has worked. Two weeks of vacation a year to start, three weeks after five years of service, and four weeks after ten years of employment is standard. However, this is an area that can often be negotiated if you have built up considerable vacation time with your prior employer.

Finally, make sure you understand how your company handles other benefits such as sick leave, emergency leave, and tuition reimbursement. You may find that your benefit program offers more than you thought.

Questions You Should Ask 18

Successful negotiation is more than simply getting the right salary offer. The money won't mean much if you don't enjoy the work you're doing. Far too many people fail to investigate exactly what they'll be doing on the job before accepting the offer.

For example, if the job carries with it a great deal of risk, you are bound to want more money, or at least a guaranteed severance package. If the job is ideal, you may be willing to settle for a little less cash. The only way to accurately assess the job is by asking the right kinds of questions. Companies will usually be quite candid with you about the joys and frustrations of the job, if you ask. Just because the information isn't volunteered doesn't mean it's not available.

Ask the Tough Questions

Individuals often don't give enough thought to the questions they should ask in the interview. They miss the opportunity to obtain valuable information that can help determine how good the fit will be between them and the employer. Applicants often feel that they will offend the company if they ask in-depth questions. Nothing could be farther from the truth. Most people ask the same old questions time after time. Managers actually are impressed by candidates who ask thought provoking questions. Asking a question that makes the interviewer think can significantly raise your stock in the interviewer's estimation. This can translate into actual dollars when it comes time to negotiate the salary.

It's very much in your self-interest to ask good, tough, probing questions. While you never want to be rude or belligerent in the interview, that doesn't mean you are limited to asking only polite questions.

Think of your pending future employer as a marriage partner. If the marriage doesn't work out down the road, who is going to be hurt more? It certainly isn't going to be the company. Thus, you want to make sure to get as much information as possible about what it's like to work for the company. Interestingly, when things don't work out, it's often for reasons you could have known about beforehand, if only you had asked the right questions.

When it comes time to ask questions in the interview, consider the following.

Why is the job open? What happened to the incumbent? A quick way to assess the risk associated with the job is to find out why the position is available. If the job is open because it is primarily a developmental assignment and the incumbent was promoted, that's a good sign. However, if the last two managers were fired for not meeting their goals, what are the odds that the same fate will befall you?

There is nothing wrong with accepting a risky assignment. However, there should be some additional benefits that will make it worth while. If you learn that the position has a history of negative turnover, use that information to negotiate a higher salary or a guaranteed severance package.

Also try to find out the answer to the related question of why the company is not filling the position from within. Does recruiting an outside candidate reflect a short-term lack of internal resources, or is management development just not very important to the company? You'll want to know the answers to these questions before you sign up.

How will my performance be measured? Nothing wrecks the employment honeymoon faster than a miscommunication between boss and subordinate about what is expected in terms of performance. Often both parties assume that they are in agreement, when in fact they aren't. This can come as a rude surprise when your salary increase doesn't reflect the contribution you thought you were making to the organization.

The solution is simple, although often overlooked. Ask that you and your boss sit down once a month during the first four to six months of your employment to discuss how you're doing. After six months, meeting once a quarter will probably be enough.

Make sure that these meetings don't fall by the wayside. In order for the meetings to accomplish their purpose they can't become casual conversations in the hallway. Misunderstandings about performance are easily correctable if caught early. Waiting six months or a year before having a candid conversation is usually fatal to the working relationship, and often your career.

What are the characteristics of people who have been successful here, and, conversely, when people have failed, what have been the common reasons? This question is one of my favorites. The reaction many managers have when they hear it is: "I've got to remember to ask that question the next time I'm interviewing."

What makes this question particularly effective is the quality of information it provides. For example, if you learn that being an effective team player is one of characteristics for success, and you know in your heart of hearts that you're basically a loner, this isn't going to be the company for you. If, however, you discover that the company puts a big emphasis on individual initiative and creativity, the lack of which was a major frustration with your previous employer, you may have found a great match.

What do people like most and least about working here? This question is a variation on the previous. Before joining the company, you'll want to know what the frustrations are in addition to the aspects that people particularly enjoy about their work environment. This is an excellent question to learn about the culture of the company and the management style so that you can determine how well you might fit in.

What's a likely career path? Where might I be in five years?   Companies vary enormously on the amount of emphasis they place on an individual's career development. In some organizations, it's a religion, while other companies pay scant attention to where any of their employees might move to once the current assignment is completed. Generally speaking, the more mature the industry, the more likely it is to have an emphasis on internal career development. High technology companies, with their boom or bust orientation, tend to be on the other end of the scale.

The more a company devotes resources to career development, the more security you're likely to have. To the extent you hear that employees have jobs, not careers, you'll know that the job comes with its fair share of risk.

How long have you been in this job?   If the boss has been in the current assignment for the past twenty years, it's safe to assume that he isn't going anywhere. That's not necessarily a negative. The question becomes: what happens to the people under him?

If the boss has a great reputation for developing people who subsequently go on to greater positions in other areas of the company, so much the better. However, if the boss's lack of movement is going to impede your advancement, that could be a problem.

What's the background of the leadership of the company?   There are usually one or two positions or functions that produce the majority of senior managers. You'll want to know what these positions and functions are, especially if you have your eye on a general management position. The "feeders" to the top slots vary considerably from industry to industry.

For example, in consumer package goods companies, such as Procter & Gamble and Kraft, the top jobs have been traditionally staffed by people out of the marketing organization. This can be of concern to someone whose background is in finance. While finance is the route to the top in many industries, it's more of a long shot as a route to the top in consumer goods.

There are certain functions, such as human resources or PR, which are staff jobs regardless of the industry. People go into these types of positions because they enjoy the work. They realize that they will probably not be the next president of the company.

For people who aspire to general manager positions, the

path is not always obvious. Make sure you know whether you're on the right track.

What is a typical day like?   This question is a little corny, although the information you get is helpful in evaluating an opportunity. It's corny because it's asked all the time, and usually there isn't any such thing as a "typical day." Nonetheless, the answer will give you a sense for the variety of work activities and how much the position interacts with other departments. Don't be surprised, however, if you see a look of boredom settle over the interviewer's face when you ask the question.

   A better way to get similar information is to request to spend a day with someone currently performing the job. This is popular with sales organizations, where spending a day in the field is a common element of the selection process. Your request can be more readily accommodated if you are applying for lower or middle management positions. Actually spending a day observing can provide you with great insights into what a "typical" day is really like.

Questions Not to Ask   Applicants still sometimes leave their common sense in their car when it comes time to ask questions. One of the common mistakes is to not have any questions prepared for the different types of interviewer you're likely to meet.

   This is especially true when you're interviewing with human resources. A common tendency is to presume that human resources doesn't have a vote, and consequently that preparing questions isn't needed. Taking the attitude that you don't have any questions that personnel could possibly answer usually backfires. While it's true that the personnel staff can't make you an offer, they are often able to derail your candidacy if they so desire. Human resources is a great opportunity to learn about culture, management style, and advancement. This is information you'll need in order to make a sound decision.

   Finally, don't raise the issue of salary and benefits in the first interview. Your goal at this stage of the process is to impress the interviewer with your background and the value you can bring to the organization. You need to accomplish this before the subject of salary comes up. If the subject is raised early, it's far too easy for the company to dismiss you as being "too expensive." You have a lot more negotiating room once you've impressed them with your accomplishments and achievements.

Questions to Expect

19

Success in salary negotiating depends on two important factors: making your prospective manager feel comfortable with you and impressing that person with the value you can bring to the company. Much of your success in salary negotiating will depend on your effectiveness in the interview.

Unfortunately, many people think that they interview better than they actually do. Many individuals believe they can sell themselves without any problems—just get them the interview. They don't practice or prepare for the interview, and consequently don't do well. The key to interview success is the same as in any other aspect of salary negotiating: practice and preparation. If you invest the time necessary, you'll do fine. Arrogantly overvaluing your capabilities will result in disappointment.

Remember, it's not enough simply to get the employment offer. Companies often give offers with a wait-and-see attitude. They want new employees to prove themselves. How likely is it that someone hired under this scenario will receive a highly competitive salary offer? In order for you to maximize the offer, you've got to impress them in the interview.

While it's impossible to completely prepare for every conceivable question you might get asked, there are a number of questions that do come up repeatedly in interviews. At a minimum, you must be fully prepared to answer these basic "blocking and tackling" questions. Let's take a look at some of the more common questions you're likely to get asked, the reasons interviewers ask them, and strategies on responding.

Tell me a little about yourself. This question is one of the most common used to kick off the interview. It's also one of the most perplexing to answer. What exactly does this person want to know? Where should I start? What should I include and what should I leave out? After all, the interviewer can't possibly want to know everything about me!

Interviewers ask this question for a variety of reasons. Sometimes it is asked just to get the ball rolling. The interviewer really is interested in getting to know you as a person. Other interviews use this question because they are uncomfortable in the interview and don't know what else to ask. It's an easy way for the interviewer to get the burden of the interview off of his or her shoulders and onto yours. As seasoned interviewers know, thinking up questions is one of the most difficult parts of the interview.

A problem for many individuals who have significant experience is how to condense fifteen to twenty years of work into a brief monologue that won't leave the interviewer bored to tears. Summarizing your life is difficult. Doing it in two minutes is a daunting task for even the most eloquent among us.

One way to answer this question is to throw back to the interviewer. You can do this by breaking down your experience into major segments and then asking which aspect of your background the interviewer would like for you to elaborate upon. For example:

> "As you can see from my resume, I have a degree in marketing and spent the first ten years of my career in advertising. About seven years ago I switched to the client side and went to work for Chicago Fine Foods as their manager of marketing. We've been successful

in realigning the sales force, developing some
innovative advertising, and increasing our
market penetration. Which aspect of may
career would you like me to talk about first?"

This tactic is often effective in getting the interviewer
to focus on a particular aspect of your background. It's always easier to handle the interview if you can divine what
kind of information the employer is looking for. However,
you need to be prepared for the retort, "I don't care, just
tell me about yourself."

Wonderful. Now you're back to square one. Since this
response is likely, you've got to be prepared and have your
life "summary" ready. This two-minute overview of your
life should still end up with the question, "What aspect of
my background can I tell you more about?"

The presentation has distinctive components. Start out
with one or two sentences on who you are and where you're
from. This helps personalize the conversation. Never forget
the saying, "Companies don't hire people. People hire people." If you don't establish a personal connection in the interview, you probably won't receive an offer or the salary
you want.

The next section of your verbal presentation briefly
summarizes your educational background. The more years
you have been out of school, the less time you should spend
on this area, unless you learn that you and the interviewer
are alumni of the same school.

Next, summarize your work history, focusing on key accomplishments rather than the reasons you became dissat-
isfied and left. Job seekers often confuse the interview with
a confessional. They approach the process as if they must
clean themselves of all past sins before their candidacy can
be evaluated. Focus on what you accomplished and how the
company was better off by having had you as an employee.
Speak of job changes simply as "better opportunities." If
the interviewer wants further information, he or she will
ask. An example of a work history summary follows.

I was born and raised in Boston. My father is
an engineer and my mother is a homemaker.
When it came time to go to college, I very much
wanted to go to school in another state, so I
applied and was accepted for early admission
at Washington University. I majored in
English, largely because of a lifetime love for
reading and writing. Upon graduation I went
to work for a small recruiting firm. I stayed

with the firm for five years, progressing from
administrative assistant to consultant to
principle. I eventually accepted an offer with a
client and joined them in Chicago as their
director of recruiting. I've been with them for
the past eight years and was fortunate to
receive a significant promotion three years ago
to head up the human resources department.
What can I tell you more about?

Since it is nearly certain that you'll get asked this question
in the interview, you must practice what you're going to
say. Your life overview should not take longer than two to
three minutes to recite. Any longer and you'll wind up bor-
ing the listener. You want to hit the high points of your career and then have the interviewer direct you to the areas
in which he or she wants more information. This will enable you to focus on the most important and relevant aspects of your background.

As mentioned previously, make sure you practice this
out loud. The more you recite the overview, the more comfortable you will be and the better your presentation.

Why did you decide to major in history?   "Why did
you?" questions are very important because they go to the
issue of judgment. Most interviewers work from the premise that the past is a strong predictor of the future. People
who have been successful in the past are likely to replicate
that success in the future. Your answer to these questions
tells the interviewer a lot about how you make decisions. If
you articulate a variety of pragmatic reasons for why you
have done what you've done, the interviewer will conclude
that you demonstrate sound judgment. If your reasons
sound frivolous, the interviewer will assume that your
decision-making capability is equally shallow.

The key to answering these question is to mention a variety of factors you considered before making your decision. If you can discuss the pros and cons of the decision
you made, so much the better. Chances are you have made
few decisions about which you feel 100 percent positive. By
discussing both sides of the issue, you will impress the interviewer with your analytical skills. For example:

> I always had been fascinated with history since
> I was little. I was encouraged by my parents to
> pursue a liberal arts degree primarily for the
> depth and breadth of education it would

provide. While I realized that the knowledge
would be highly beneficial, it might not
directly translate into a job upon graduation.
That was a risk I knew I was taking. However,
in hindsight I'm glad I made the decision I did.
The study of history gave me a perspective on
the past which I think will be helpful to me in
making business decisions. Additionally, it
strengthened my analytical skills and
improved my writing.

Your answer should be positive yet pragmatic. You can
anticipate that a bulk of the questions you are asked in the
interview will be in the "why did you?" vein. Again, preparation is important. Go over your resume and highlight
each significant turning point in your life. Include the reasons why you attended the schools you went to, the jobs you
had, and the extracurricular activities you participated in.
For each time you faced a fork in the road, be prepared to
explain why you went down one road and not the other.

You also need to be prepared for the interviewer who
approaches your life decisions from the perspective of "why
didn't you?" This negative form of questioning forces you
to articulate confidence in your career choice. For example,
it is not uncommon to be asked a question such as "Why
didn't you major in accounting?" Now you are faced with
explaining not only why history was a good choice, but also
why you did not choose accounting.

This type of question is tricky, because the interviewer
often has a hidden agenda. There's a reason why the interviewer chooses accounting to ask you about. The interviewer may have majored in accounting, or perhaps it is
the educational background of other successful people in
the department. Thus, when you are asked to defend a decision you didn't make, don't make negative remarks
about the alternative.

Discuss your decision from a positive viewpoint. Explain why the decision you made was right for you. For example:

Certainly a degree in accounting would have
greatly assisted me for this type of career. I
enjoyed the two accounting classes I took and
sometimes wish I had taken more. However,
for me the degree in history wound up being a
good decision. It developed my analytical
skills, which I think is another important
criteria for success in this job.

By striking this type of balance you will be able to turn a potentially negative question into a positive answer.

What are your strengths and weaknesses? Obviously, the first part of this question is easier to answer than the second part, Although this isn't a particularly good interview question, it has become a standard, so you had best be prepared.

The reason it's not a very good question is that no one is really going to confess to some terrible sin. It's unlikely that anyone would say, "Well, I guess that one of my weaknesses is that I just don't like people—and I'm lazy."

One reason interviewers ask this question so frequently is that they remember being asked the question when they were applying for a job and having difficulty answering it. The question has become something of an initiation rite.

The strategy for answering this question is to break it down into two parts. A problem some people have with answering the first part of the question is a reluctance to speak about their strengths. People are often afraid of coming across as being a braggart or too cocky. As a result, they overcompensate and hide their light under the proverbial bushel.

You can make yourself feel more comfortable in answering this question by distancing yourself from the answer. Instead of saying what *you* think your strengths are, discuss what your boss would say. "In terms of my strengths, I think that if you asked my boss, he would say that I was particularly effective in initiative and follow through." Most interviewers won't mind if you answer the question from this perspective, and you are less likely to feel like you are bragging.

Give specific examples to back up your claims. It's not enough to simply say your strength is initiative. You've got to provide an example if you really want to convince the interviewer. There is a world of difference between saying something is a strength and proving it by example. By seeding your interview with real-life stories and anecdotes, you will come across more favorably and are less likely to be forgotten as a candidate.

This last point is very important. Companies usually interview a large group of people, which is then narrowed down to a small number of final candidates. Although you probably won't embarrass yourself in the interview, the odds of being just another candidate are very high. It's easy to be forgotten.

Using stories in your interview reduces the chance of

this happening. The reason has to do with one of the major principles of adult education. Adults don't remember facts—they remember examples. If you state that your strength is initiative without elaborating on your point with an example, the interviewer may not remember the strength, or you, for very long. Alternatively, if you give specific examples of situations where you demonstrated this skill, you greatly increase your chances of standing out from the pack. The following demonstrates a statement followed up by an example:

> My boss would probably say my major strength was initiative. I think he would say that because about two years ago I discovered we were facing a situation where prospective customers were not being contacted again for over a year. I developed and implemented a system so that accounts were called on a bimonthly basis, which increased our overall sales and ensured that potential future clients didn't slip through the cracks.

Where do you see yourself in five years?   This question is asked to determine how much you know about the particular industry and to assess how realistic you are about career growth.

The more you research your industry, the better equipped you'll be to handle this question. Some careers, such as brand management in the consumer goods industry, have clearly defined career paths and schedules for promotion. After five years with a company such as Kraft or Procter & Gamble, an individual should be at the brand-manager level where he or she is responsible for all the marketing activities for a particular product. If you are able to specifically articulate the type of position you could expect to be in after five years of successful performance, you will impress the interviewer with your knowledge of the industry.

However, many jobs are not so clearly spelled out. This is especially true of small businesses. Where you could be in five years is anyone's guess. In this day and age of corporate takeovers and mergers, even the most carefully planned career paths are often turned upside down. A safe answer in this situation would be that in five years you expect to either to have responsibility for a significant portion of a major project or be supervising 1–3 junior workers. This type of answer positions you as having goals but not being unrealistic in your expectations.

Unrealistic career expectations are a cause of concern for many employers. This is especially true for companies which recruit on graduate business school campuses. Recruiting is a difficult and time-consuming process. Once the candidate is on board, the last thing the company wants to have happen is for him or her to leave. If the individual and the company aren't in sync on career progression, it is likely that the marriage will be short-lived. Thus it is in your own best interest to research the company to determine if you can live with where your career is likely to be in five years.

We are interviewing a large number of candidates for this position. Why should we hire you?   This question is typically asked at the end of the interview. Its purpose is to determine both how stiff your backbone is and how confident you are about your skills. This question is a favorite of sales-driven organizations.

This question can come as a little bit of a shock if you're not prepared. Its bluntness can be unsettling. If you maintain your composure, however, you'll do fine.

The basic answer to this question runs as follows: "Because there is a good fit between what you are looking for and my skills." You'll need to elaborate, of course, but that should be your basic theme.

This is a good interview question from the company's perspective because it quickly eliminates those with little confidence or who really don't have the necessary skills. Both of these groups fold under the pressure. Once again, careful preparation will ensure success.

Think about this question from the perspective of the company. What do you think they need in an individual? What types of skills and traits will be important? Do you have those skills? If not, save yourself the time and effort and don't even bother to interview.

If you do have the skills, how do you know? When have you demonstrated them? Can you provide specific examples? Practice articulating these stories out loud. Preparing in this manner will enable you to hit this question for a home run when it's pitched at you.

Finally, there is no way you can predict every question that you may be asked. There is no accounting for the oddball interviewer who may ask: "If you were a car, what type of car would you be?"

But although you can't prepare for every question, you still have no excuse for being as prepared as possible. Think of your resume as the playing field. Everything that is on that sheet of paper is likely to be asked in the interview. Think of the questions you would ask if you were interviewing the person in the resume. What would you want to know more about? What would be your concerns?

In order to successfully negotiate a new job, you will have to clear the interview hurdle. As in all other aspects of successful negotiations, preparation and practice are what separates the winners from the losers.

Negotiating an Employment Contract

Employment contracts are the stuff of lore and legend. Many people, particularly senior-level executives, wonder if they should negotiate to get one. Although employment contracts receive much attention in the press, they are in fact quite rare; only a very small percentage of executives receive them.

Many companies are opposed to giving their managers contracts. They believe it violates the spirit of employment arrangements. The company's position is that although they have extensively interviewed you and checked your references prior to making you an offer, they're still taking a risk. You may interview much better than you perform. Many experienced managers have been burned once or twice by hiring someone who "just didn't work out." As the old saying goes—"once burned, twice shy." Although the manager may fervently hope you prove to be a star, the manager wants an out if you don't meet expectations. Thus, most managers are very leery of offering contracts.

The Employment Relationship   Contracts also go against the philosophy of "employment at will," which governs employment law in most states. The concept is straightforward. The employer can fire you, or you can quit, if either of you grows tired of the relationship. Over the years, laws have been enacted to prevent employers from firing us simply because we get old; conversely, we may be precluded from going to work for a direct competitor if we sign such an agreement with our employer. This freedom and protection under the law is viewed by many employers as all the contract that is necessary.

Although employment contracts are rare, employment agreements are not. However, if you are presented with an employment agreement, make sure you negotiate it. If your employer doesn't offer you a written employment agreement, make sure you get one before resigning from your old job. While the term "contract" may frighten off employers, a written agreement can be much less threatening. Interestingly, a written employment agreement will usually provide you with as much legal protection as any contract.

Employment agreements that are initiated and presented to you by the company are notoriously one-sided. In effect, most of them are simply non-compete agreements. A standard non-compete agreement bars you from working for a competitor within a certain geographic radius for a certain period of time if you leave the company voluntarily. One year and a 50-mile radius is standard. These agreements are most common in sales organizations. However, the use of non-compete agreements has expanded in recent years to cover a large number of workers who have proprietary knowledge about a company's operations. As business becomes increasingly competitive, the use of these agreements is likely to rise.

Not surprisingly, these agreements have been hotly contested in court. Individuals have argued that the agreements prevent them from gainfully earning a living. Employers say that the agreements were entered into voluntarily and, since the employee left of his or her own free will, the agreement should be upheld. Since the courts tend to side with employers on this issue, you'll want to be very careful and thoroughly review any document before you sign.

Non-compete Agreements

However, non-compete agreements offer you an intriguing opportunity to negotiate. In fact, you may be able to reap the benefits of an employment contract. When most people think about why they want an employment contract, the answer usually is security. They view the contract as a method of guaranteeing income. This objective can also be achieved through the employment agreement.

When you are presented with the employment agreement and/or non-compete letter, agree to sign it if the company will commit to paying you a guaranteed amount of severance if they decide to terminate your employment. The company may initially balk at this, often because they have never done it before. You need to be prepared to explain that this addition to the document makes the agreement more fair to both parties. You're willing to forego working for a competitor, and they're willing to pay you a specified amount of severance. They may balk at the concept of guaranteed severance; we'll discuss a method of getting around that objection shortly.

If the company does not initiate a written agreement make sure that you do. Always get the details of your employment arrangement down on paper before quitting your current job. Even in environments where deals are "struck by handshakes" and a "man's word is his bond," people leave, die, and sometimes forget. Make sure you've got written confirmation of the verbal agreement.

Severance

While you shouldn't hesitate to bring up the subject of severance, don't be surprised if some companies are reluctant to formally offer you a guaranteed severance package. Part of their reluctance, however, may be semantics. Companies don't like "contracts" but they are usually willing to provide "employment agreements." Guaranteed "severance" may cause nervousness; talk instead about stipulating an "extended notice." This negotiating tool is frequently used in academia, and its use has spread into the private sector. If the company wants to terminate your employment, they must give you a specified period of notice, such as four months, or keep you on the payroll for the same amount of time.

Extended notice or severance agreements are particularly important if you are accepting a risky position. The definition of a risky opportunity *can* vary. It may be a company in financial trouble or negatively affected by the economy. Risk does not have to be thought of in purely financial terms, however. Your prospective boss may appear to be difficult to get along with, or you may discover that the last three people in the job were fired. The greater the likelihood that things won't work out, the more important it is that you have a severance agreement negotiated in advance.

Put It in Writing!

Most employers won't object to putting the employment agreement in writing. An offer letter is standard practice, especially for larger companies. What many often overlook is an acceptance letter. The offer letter outlines what the company proposes. The acceptance letter reviews exactly what the two of you agreed upon. The differences can be substantial.

It's in your best interest to write the initial draft of the acceptance letter yourself. Whoever pens the document has the most influence on what goes in it. You want to make sure that important points are not intentionally or unintentionally left out. In this letter you'll want to include such elements as reporting relationships, job title, scope of responsibility, base salary, bonus participation (including a negotiated guaranteed first year's bonus), signing bonus, relocation allowance, perks such as car allowances and country club membership, and the severance arrangement.

It's a little inappropriate for you to ask the company to sign a copy of your letter, so you'll need to end your acceptance letter by saying, "I would appreciate your confirming these arrangements in writing." If these are the points that you and the company have agreed upon there shouldn't be any problem with the company confirming the arrangements in writing.

Employment contracts are hard to come by and few companies will offer you one. Written employment agreements are much easier to obtain and are as effective as a contract. Remember, don't resign your current position until you have all the details of the new position confirmed in writing.

Salary Negotiating for the Self-Employed

Salary negotiating for the self-employed poses its own unique challenges. Corporate restructurings and downsizings have sent thousands of former company managers into the ranks of the self-employed. Many have started up small consulting practices, often as a sole proprietor. Since setting consulting fees is a form of salary negotiating, it's worth spending some time examining how you can best get maximum dollar for your services.

Consulting Fees   Setting fees as a consultant is more art than science. Even consultants working for the largest of consulting firms will admit that what they charge varies enormously. To a certain extent, fees are charged based on what the consultant thinks the client will pay. Although that is not the best method for establishing a fee structure, it is not uncommon. What you charge as a consultant will be based primarily on two factors: (1) What you want to earn and (2) what other consultants offering similar services are charging. Setting your fee is similar to any other negotiating process. Your ultimate success depends on the quality of the homework you do.

The first step in determining what other consulting firms are charging is to find out who the other firms are working in your field. Head to your nearest public library and ask to speak to the research librarian. Research librarians are a woefully underutilized resource. They exist to help people in their research projects, yet many people are unaware of their existence.

Ask the research librarian for the directories of consulting firms. Most libraries keep more than one in their reference collection. Directories are indexed by functions, by industries, and by location. Unless you are providing an extremely esoteric service, you should be able to identify a number of your competitors. Identifying six to eight firms should suffice for your purposes.

The next step is to find out how much these firms charge for their services. Ideally, you'll discover that you have a friend who works at one of these firms—rather unlikely. Since most firms are protective about their fees, you'll have to use a little subterfuge in order to find out what they charge.

One method some consultants use is to pose as a potential buyer of their service. Another ploy is to have a friend who works for a company that might have a legitimate need for the services make a call to the consultant. Using one of these two methods, new consultants are often able to determine how much companies are willing to pay for these services.

Another alternative is to review some of the surveys on consulting fees which are available. One of the best is produced by Howard Shenson's organization. His book, *The Contract and Fee-Setting Guide for Consultants,* is considered one of the best reference sources for consultants on this subject.

Most consultants charge on an hourly or daily basis. Consulting advisor Shenson says the average daily billing rate for most consultants is $929. The amount you'll be able to charge, however, will vary considerably. Even though the daily fee may seem considerable, it's important to remember that consultants usually aren't able to work every day, and taxes, expenses, and other costs must be paid out of the fee.

Getting the Pay of a Full-Timer

Many consultants set a financial goal of earning as much as they did in their previous job. A method of calculating the hourly billing rate you'll need to achieve this goal is to take your current salary and divide it by 52. Divide this number by 40 and multiply it by 2.5. This accounts for the fact that a typical consultant only bills 12 to 14 days per month. Round your final answer up to a number divisible by five.

For example, if your last salary was $40,000, you would divide it by 52 ($769) and again by 40 ($19). Multiply this by 2.5 ($47) and round up to the nearest number divisible by five ($50). Thus, $50 is your hourly billing rate.

On the surface, the thought of consulting can be very appealing: no boss, unlimited income opportunity, and the ability to pick and choose clients. But the image of a carefree life spent advising companies on how to solve business problems has little to do with the realities of becoming an independent consultant. In fact, a recent survey computed that the average first-year earnings for new independent consultants was about $12,000.

Success in independent consulting is not dependent solely on technical competence. Expertise in a particular field is important, but competence by itself is not enough for success. Most beginning consultants don't realize how difficult it is to get clients. The ability to market your services is as important as your technical skills are for achieving the financial success you want.

Anyone considering becoming an independent consultant should consider the range of services that they will offer. It's important to develop a portfolio of consulting expertise that you can market. Successful consultants maintain a balance between offering too few services and too many. It's also important to identify the functional skills you possess and the specialized knowledge you have about a particular industry.

A salesman in the electronics industry, for example, could provide consulting assistance on trends in electronics, a report on what customers look for in electronic suppliers, an analysis on why a client purchased a competitor's product or development of a training program on improving sales skills. A personnel manager could provide advice on compensation, training, implementing a benefits program, or recruiting.

Successful consultants agree that the first step in marketing your service is to determine whether your potential clients will be corporations, individuals, or both. Many times a former employer provides the initial consulting assignment. Making random phone calls to companies is usually not very effective.

If your expertise is technically oriented, develop a list of other companies in your field. If your knowledge is more general, you may find that you can successfully sell your services to a wide range of clients outside your particular industry.

Self-Marketing

The key to successfully marketing your consulting services is to become highly visible as an expert to your targeted group of potential clients. Two of the most effective methods are writing and publishing articles on your subject of expertise and speaking before groups of potential clients. Although you usually won't get paid for these presentations, they can pay off substantially down the road.

Check the public library for the *Encyclopedia of Associations,* which includes a list of trade groups active in your field. Write the local program director and offer to speak at the next meeting. Find out if the association publishes a newsletter; if so, submit an article. Find out which trade publications your potential clients read and submit articles to those.

Even the most successful independent consultants know that they cannot predict their level of activity and income beyond a few months. Although you may be overwhelmed with work today, three months down the road you may be without an assignment. Thus it is critical that you keep your fixed expenses as low as possible. Knowing that you have three to six months worth of living expenses in the bank can give you the confidence to keep going when you experience a temporary lack of assignments.

Although independent consulting can provide enormous career satisfaction and independence, it is a little like being a circus performer who works without a net. Consulting usually is an option best suited to those who are stout of heart and have a skill that can be readily marketed.

Effective
Telephone Skills

It cannot be stressed enough that successful negotiations depend on effective communication skills. One of the most powerful weapons in the salary negotiator's arsenal is the telephone. However, even the most self-confident of individuals are prone to an outbreak of nerves when having to talk to a prospective employer on the phone. Often people feel that they are intruding when they initiate the call, or feel unprepared when they are the recipient. In this day of voice mail and answering machines, actually making contact with a real human being can become a challenge.

Since making a good impression on the phone is critical for negotiating success, here are some suggestions on mastering the telephone.

Speak Clearly   Although it would seem obvious, in order to be effective on the telephone you have to be heard. Tucking the phone under your chin or holding the receiver out of line with your mouth dramatically reduces the clarity and impact of your words. If you are soft-spoken, hold the phone directly in front of your mouth during your opening statement. You don't need to hold the receiver close to your ear during the first few seconds when you are talking.

Have your opening statement prepared and practiced. There is a world of difference between thinking about how you will say something and actually articulating it. Practice by rehearsing with a friend or while driving in the car. Practicing will increase your self-confidence and the impact of your delivery. Your voice should project a pleasant, personable personality rather than appearing timid or overly aggressive. By recording yourself on tape, you can help yourself learn how you are coming across.

When making a cold call to someone you don't know, keep in mind that you are likely to have no more than five minutes to make your case. Thus, you want to make every statement count. Telephone sales pros suggest speaking for no more than forty seconds at a time and to pause briefly after making an important point.

Introducing Yourself   An introductory statement might go as follows:

> Good morning, Mr. James. My name is Mark Satterfield and a mutual associate of ours, Bill Brown, thought that my experience selling computers might be of benefit to your company. Is this a convenient time to talk?

One of the more common errors people make on the phone is forgetting to ask whether the listener has time to talk. If the answer is no, ask when a convenient time would be to call the person back. Try to avoid having the individual call you back. That puts you in the uncomfortable situation of not knowing when the call will be returned.

Return Calls   As much as you want to initiate rather than receive calls, having to receive return calls is a fact of life. The problem is that return calls may come without any warning and catch you by surprise. The carefully prepared opening remark flies out of your mind as you frantically try to remember who you're talking to and what aspect of your background you most wanted to discuss. To buy yourself time, try saying the following: "Thanks very much for returning my call, Mr. Smith. Let me put you on hold for just a moment while I change phones." This tactic allows you to collect your thoughts or quickly review some notes made in anticipation of the call.

Keeping track of everyone you've called can become quite unwieldy very quickly. The problem becomes worse if it takes several days before you finally connect with your prospect. To keep your memory sharp, maintain a detailed call list of everyone you're trying to contact. Update it daily so the names are quickly identifiable. Remember, you will only have a few seconds to "change phones," which does not give you a great amount of time to refresh your memory.

Style   People who sell products over the phone also recommend that you tailor your speaking style to the person you are calling. If the individual speaks quickly and directly, use short, concise statements. Conversely, if your caller's style is relaxed and friendly, adopt a more personable speaking tone.

Answering machines are a fact of life. Be aware that most people dislike listening to a long message, so keep your own recording brief and to the point:

> Hello, you have reached 234-5555. I'm, sorry
> I'm not here to personally take your call, but
> please leave a message at the tone and I'll
> return your call as soon as possible.

Make sure that the tone of the message is friendly and conveys the impression that you are in fact sorry to have missed the call.

When leaving a message on someone's answering machine, explain why you are calling. This ensures that your call is not mistaken for that of the ubiquitous mutual fund salesperson.

> Good morning this is Mark Satterfield. I was
> following up of my letter of October 10th which
> was prompted by our mutual associate Bill

Jones. I can be reached at 234-5555 until five today or 235-7777 after 6:00 pm. I look forward to speaking with you soon.

Tenacity is critical for success in telephoning. Unfortunately, the likelihood of actually reaching your prospect on the first call is slim. Playing "telephone tag," while frustrating is unavoidable. However, I have discovered when I have finally made the connection after repeated attempts, my caller often comments positively on my persistence. Never has a speaker indicated that they were put off by repeated messages. Thus, with the telephone, as with all aspects of the negotiating process, err on the side of assertiveness.

The Salary Negotiation Meeting

It's a given that you'll be nervous in the salary negotiation meeting. Nervousness affects each of us differently. Some people sweat, others develop a case of dry mouth, while others twitch, jerk, or display other unsightly mannerisms.

Nervousness can also affect short-term memory. In tense situations remembering the name of your lifelong best friend can become a problem. Nothing is worse than spending hours preparing for the important meeting only to forget the points you wanted to make. Since relying on our memory in a negotiation meeting is problematic, you may well ask whether you should refer to notes during the meeting.

The answer is, it depends. Overall, you are better off working without notes if possible. You will be perceived more professionally and appear more confident if your presentation is seemingly extemporaneous. Some interviewers regard looking at notes in the interview as negative, while others don't seem to be overly affected by it. However, it's clear that you're better off if you can work without the cue cards.

Appearances While some negotiators may look at you as less professional if you rely on notes, the alternative can be worse. Drawing a blank in the meeting is both embarrassing and probably fatal to success. Thus, you may wish to strive for a compromise. Have notes available but don't refer to them unless absolutely necessary.

Preparation The first step in preparing to take notes is purchasing a suitable pad on which notes can be taken and referred to in a professional manner. Although a pad of lined paper fulfills the functional requirements, it doesn't convey the professional image you need to create. You will want to invest in a binder of either leather or vinyl in which to put the pad. Binders are readily available at office supply stores, grocery stores, or your local variety store. You may even own a few already. Binders are a popular giveaway at many corporate functions. However, make sure that the binder you bring to the meeting doesn't have your former company's logo emblazoned on the front. This is tacky, and it establishes you as a lower-level player.

Although you want to look professional, you don't need to spend a lot of money on the binder. Vinyl is as suitable as leather and costs significantly less. The color of your binder should complement your briefcase, wallet, and other professional accessories. Burgundy or black is the best choice for most people.

One of the most difficult parts of the meeting will be when it comes time for you to state what you want and why you think you deserve it. Answering these questions requires knowledge of salary trends and other statistical information, which can be hard to memorize. This is when your memory is most likely to fail you, and when your notes will come in the most handy. Prepare for this situation by writing on the first page of the tablet in your binder the justifications for your salary request. Use an ink color which stands out, and print your cues twice the space you normally would. You want to be able to quickly gaze at your notes and read the information. You *don't* want to spend a lot of time trying to decipher your own handwriting. Remember that the purpose of these notes is to jog your memory; thus, they should be written in a form that is quickly and easily read.

You'll also want to invest in a high-quality writing instrument. Nothing soils the image of professionalism quicker than producing a well-chewed-on Bic pen to take notes. An investment of $25–$50 will provide you with a writing instrument that complements the look you are cultivating; you don't need to spend $100 on a Mont Blanc pen. Remember that no one is going to pay you the salary you seek unless you convey the image of success. While you don't have to go overboard, developing the cultivated look of a professional will pay off and increase your overall value. If you want to earn big money, you have to look like you deserve to earn it.

The Meeting Should you take notes during the meeting? In certain instances this is perfectly acceptable. As a general rule, however, you should try to commit as much as possible to memory and minimize madly scribbling whenever possible. However, when details of the offer are given, it makes enormous sense to write them down. This also indicates that you are taking the offer seriously and reduces the chances that the opponent will later modify their stance.

Aside from specific offer amounts, it's best not to take a lot of notes during the meeting. You tend to come across more as a reporter than a negotiator, and scribbling takes away from the natural give-and-take of the negotiating process.

Once you have left the meeting, immediately write down the points that were discussed. List what was agreed upon and what was left unresolved. You may think that you will remember the conversation, but you probably won't. Our memories are very focused on the short term. You will be very frustrated if you try to recall the conversation after a number of weeks have passed. Thus, it is very important that you sit down as soon as possible after the meeting and commit to paper as much as you can remember.

Written Communication

24

In order to become an effective negotiator you will also have to become a good writer. Too many individuals are intimidated by putting their thoughts down in writing and thus try to avoid the process whenever possible.

Job Searching Negotiating usually takes a number of steps. For instance, if you plan on negotiating with a new employer for a larger salary, you will first have to obtain an interview. Many managers don't respond favorably to a cold call. They prefer that you write them first to explain why a meeting would be beneficial. Once you have the meeting, you'll want to follow up with a note reiterating specific points of the conversation. Finally, once the deal is concluded, you will want to write your new manager a letter accepting the offer.

Many people who have difficulty in putting their thoughts down on paper were told at one point in time that they either didn't write well or suffered from using poor grammar. The rules governing proper writing can be highly confusing. Even experienced writers often have difficulty in differentiating a dangling participle from a preposition.

Nonetheless, your ability to conduct a successful job search and salary negotiation will be enhanced if you master the fundamentals of effective job search correspondence. Too often individuals shoot themselves in the foot by sending letters that are poorly written. Ideally, your letter should read as if you were speaking. If the letter sounds awkward when read aloud, you probably need to rewrite.

Try to keep your letter to one page. Your correspondence should cover three points: Why you are writing, why a meeting would be mutually beneficial, and the date and time you plan to follow up. This last point is important. Don't end your letter by saying, "Please feel free to contact me at my home address to arrange a meeting at your convenience." This rather weak closing will usually not elicit a positive response. Rather, close your job search letters with an active statement, such as "I will call you Thursday morning to arrange a meeting at your convenience."

You will need to become proficient in writing a number of different types of letters, including cover letters, requests for an informational meeting, follow-up notes, and thank-you letters. Let's look at examples of each.

Cover Letter   The cover letter normally accompanies your resume. Its purpose is to pave the way for a future meeting. An example of an effective cover letter follows:

> A mutual associate, Ms. Susan Smith of XYZ Company, suggested that I contact you. I am in the process of changing careers and am focusing on the field of food marketing.
>
> I have most recently worked with the advertising firm of Smith & James. As a member of the food marketing account team, we designed a marketing study to track the effect of direct mail advertising on consumer spending. This project was completed under budget and on schedule, and should play an important role in enabling the client to increase market share.

I am confident that I can make a contribution to the goals of your marketing department. I will call you the week of January 5th to determine if an interview can be arranged.

Letter Requesting an Informational Interview

The purpose of an informational interview letter is to arrange a meeting for you to learn more about a particular job or company. Try to be creative in identifying people who are experts in their field. You will find that many people are flattered when asked to talk about what they do for a living. An example follows:

> I read recently in the Journal Constitution of your promotion to Vice President. Congratulations. I wish you much continued success.
>
> I am currently in the process of investigating some new career avenues. After a great amount of thought, I have narrowed down my search to the commercial banking industry.
>
> To further prepare myself, I am hoping to have the opportunity to speak personally with professionals in the field. I would greatly appreciate it if you would be able to spare a half hour to answer a few questions I have about careers in banking.
>
> I will call you next Monday to determine a mutually convenient time when we might meet.

Follow-Up Note

The follow-up note serves to remind the reader about your visit and subtly nudge him or her along the continuing path of negotiations. Too often good intentions fall by the wayside unless you remind the person what the next steps agreed upon were.

> I enjoyed our discussion yesterday about the role I could potentially play in your organization. My background in developing point-of-sale material would be a good addition to the skills currently held by your marketing team.

As we discussed, the next step would be for me to meet with your Vice President of Marketing, Janet Smith. Your office was going to arrange the day and time of the meeting. Since I'm sometimes difficult to reach, I'll touch base with your secretary at the end of the week.

I look forward to talking with you further.

Thank You Letter

The thank-you letter serves two purposes. It is both a sign of courtesy and an effective means by which to reiterate an aspect of your background that closely relates to the needs of the employer.

I enjoyed our conversation yesterday and was pleased to have the opportunity to discuss my background with you. The marketing analyst position is very interesting, and would represent a good utilization of my education and previous work experience.

As you may recall, I recently completed a marketing study on the tire industry. Our conclusion that safety is the most compelling reason why people buy tires mirrors the theme of your current marketing campaign. I believe my skills demonstrated in preparing the study would make me a successful marketing analyst.

I look forward to continuing our discussion.

Make sure that your letters are persuasive and convey your enthusiasm for the opportunity. If you are successful, you will have gained a significant competitive advantage.

Negotiating with Universities and Colleges

As thousands of businesses have reorganized and laid off employees, many individuals find that careers in the not-for-profit sector are becoming more appealing. One area many business people are investigating are colleges and universities. There is a perception that working at a university might offer a life-style free from the competitive pressures found in industry. Additionally, many people find the prospect of actually working on a campus to be very attractive.

Academia University and college jobs offer some unique salary negotiating opportunities. You should know that you are not likely to be offered a salary competitive with what you could earn in private industry. However, there are a number of options worth discussing with the dean prior to entering the world of academia.

First, let's discuss what type of job you might go after and how you can learn about all of the available opportunities.

Unless you have a Ph.d., you probably won't be able to become a tenure-tracked faculty member. That doesn't mean that teaching is entirely out of the question. Some colleges, particularly business schools, are increasingly using experienced business people to teach certain classes such as accounting and marketing. However, you may find it difficult to support yourself just by adjunct teaching.

Most of the jobs in academia available to non-academics are in the school's administration, either working with students or being involved in the business aspects of running a school. Jobs that involve students include admissions, placement, housing, and campus life. Universities are also large businesses and require the services of accountants, data processing personnel, and human resource managers. Every university receives much of its money through gifts and has a large development staff that coordinates all fund-raising efforts.

Availability and Competition

Colleges and universities are very sensitive to ensuring that personnel openings are widely publicized. Most schools post currently available jobs on a bulletin board usually located near the personnel office. The magazine *Chronicle of Higher Education* also publishes a weekly list of openings in colleges nationwide.

If you are considering pursuing a career in academia, you need to decide between public and private institutions. Although there may be more opportunities at a large public state school, the jobs are likely to pay significantly less than their private-school counterparts. Additionally, public schools are bound by many state and federal laws that may impact the type of deal you can negotiate. In terms of compensation, private institutions are usually a better bet.

Most universities use relatively unsophisticated methods to evaluate jobs. Lower-level positions usually have established salary ranges, while higher-level administrative jobs often do not. The person who decides how much money to offer candidates is usually the dean of the school rather than the human resources department. The dean's offer will be based largely on what the person holding the position previously earned, and what other people on the dean's staff earn. The starting salaries for similar jobs can vary enormously from university to university. If the dean comes out of industry rather than academia, you have an even better chance to negotiate a respectable salary, since the dean will be most familiar with salaries paid in the private sector. Overall, salary levels are highly negotiable, especially for administrative posts at the level of director or higher.

While salaries may be negotiable, you can forget about negotiating for bonuses and stock options. There aren't any. Your base salary is the only financial component you'll receive. And remember, your increases will be in the form of percentages, so the most important number to negotiate is the initial salary.

Don't Count on Taking Summers Off

While universities don't have bonuses, they do have time off. School is in session for only nine months of the year, which can open up intriguing negotiating opportunities. However, don't assume that when the students have time off, you also will have time off. Some functions, such as those in the accounting department continue, whether the students are present or not. You must determine whether the position is a nine- or twelve-month job. However, most members of the administration at a school come from the academic side, and former professors are trained to think in nine month cycles. You can use this to your advantage.

You might try to negotiate to take the summer off for leisure or money making ventures. Jobs that revolve around providing services to students are the best candidates for this type of request. For example, the placement director's work for the year is usually completed shortly after graduation. This job might easily fit into a nine-month cycle.

While many college or university deans won't let you take an entire summer off, or the nature of the work may make it infeasible, you should negotiate vacations aggressively. A minimum vacation of one month should be your goal. The dean, particularly at private colleges, has great discretion in allowing members of the staff time off, especially those with senior-level administrative jobs.

Consulting

You can significantly augment your income if the dean will allow you to consult on the side. Many deans will be quite comfortable with letting you do so. Colleges and universities encourage their faculty to consult, since they believe it keeps them fresh and on the cutting edge of developments in their field. It also helps them supplement their income.

The same argument can be used for administrative positions. For example, the placement director might consult with companies on how to more effectively recruit on campus. The director would benefit from learning more about recruiting practices of companies and might persuade the client company to come to the director's school to recruit. Thus both the director and the school would benefit.

When approaching the dean about permission to consult, make sure you stress that your activities will not represent a conflict of interest with the school. For example, the dean would not want the placement director to set up an employment agency on the side. You'll also need to negotiate how much time during the academic year you can devote to consulting. The standard for professors is four to six days per month.

Try to avoid entering into an agreement where you will consult only when school is not in session. You may find it difficult to predict exactly when a consulting opportunity will occur, and you could severely shortchange yourself under such an arrangement. You can overcome objections by stressing the synergies that exist between your full-time job and consulting.

Whatever agreement you reach, make sure you keep it confidential. With the high cost of tuition today, students aren't likely to be thrilled that you are not devoting 100 percent of your time to their needs. However, given the generally positive attitude on most campuses toward consulting, you are likely to receive permission from the dean. The key is to position your consulting practice as being mutually beneficial to both yourself and the school.

Teaching

You might also negotiate an agreement to teach a class. This can be both fun and financially rewarding. Colleges often have to scramble in order to find a qualified person to teach classes if more students have enrolled than were predicted. This is particularly the case in business schools. Individuals with a real-world perspective are often highly valued as teachers, especially in some of the introductory or survey business courses. Fees vary from $300 to $3,000 per course per semester.

You may be qualified to teach in the adult development programs conducted in the evenings at many schools. These programs are usually run by the department of continuing education. Obtain a catalogue and see if a class is currently being offered in your area of expertise. If not, write to the program chairperson and describe your proposed program. Most classes run one night a week for three to six weeks. You are responsible for course content and handouts. The school handles the marketing of the program. You should be able to negotiate an arrangement where you split the student fees evenly.

Benefits   Benefit programs aren't usually negotiable at universities but are often quite good. Ask your dean if the school participates in the TIAA/CREF pension program. This program is one of the most financially rewarding retirement programs in any industry. Under the rules, for every dollar you put into the program, the university puts in two. You can invest up to around 5 percent of your salary. It doesn't take a mathematician to figure out that this retirement nest egg can grow quite quickly.

Universities and colleges offer some unique opportunities for individuals who have grown tired of the corporate rat race. However, the assumption that there is no money to be made in academia is not entirely true. There's more flexibility and opportunity for the effective salary negotiator than initially meets the eye.

Conveying the Image of Success

If you are going to successfully negotiate a top compensation package for yourself, you not only have to clearly articulate your accomplishments and achievements, you also have to convey the image of success. Although appearances can be deceiving and ideally more emphasis is put on substance, how you look will affect how people perceive you. The more you look like a million bucks, the more likely you are to be paid a commensurate amount. Let's examine what the successful business person wears and some of the common pitfalls of business dress.

The popularity of John Malloy's book *Dress for Success* a few years ago underscored the importance of proper business attire. If you follow some basic rules for business attire, you'll achieve the impression you want.

Advice for Men

The key point is to fit into your surroundings. You neither want to overdress nor underdress compared to the people you work with. Look to the next level in the organization for guidance. That is the dress code you should emulate. If your boss dresses like a slob but her peers are neatly turned out, you are better off by following the example of the majority. Ideally, you want to dress so that no one really remembers what you had on. Wearing a $1,500 suit in a short-sleeve-shirt environment is as inappropriate as wearing khakis if you work in a bank.

Regardless of whether you wear a suit to work or dress more casually, make sure that your clothes are clean and neatly pressed. There is a big difference between being neatly dressed and looking unkempt. Even if jeans are allowed in your place of work, you're better off by wearing casual slacks rather than Levis.

If suits are the norm in your business, start your wardrobe off with a solid navy and dark grey suit. You'll be able to achieve a number of different looks by wearing different shirts and ties. The only person who came close to looking good in a brown suit was Ronald Reagan. Brown just isn't a power color. Stick with grey and navy blue. Solid suits tend to be more versatile than pinstripes and require less effort at color coordination.

Your suit should be no more than 40 percent synthetic fiber with the remainder wool. A higher concentration of synthetics will make the suit become shiny after a few trips to the dry cleaners. (A polyester suit will melt when exposed to open flame!) Also, stay away from corduroy suits, which look great on department store mannequins and on nobody else. When buying a suit, make sure you bring with you all of the wallets, billfolds, and keys that you normally carry in your pockets. It doesn't make any sense to have your suit perfectly tailored only to discover that the suit looks lumpy when you add the typical items you carry. Put all of that stuff in your pockets *before* the tailor goes to work.

If you wear a suit, make sure you wear a long-sleeve shirt. Suit coats are typically tailored so that a half-inch of shirt cuff shows. If you wear a short-sleeve shirt under a suit jacket, it looks as if your suit has been badly tailored or that the arms have shrunk. Neither impression is good for your image.

Dress shirts should be a blend of 80 percent cotton and 20 percent polyester. Although a 100 percent cotton shirt will feel good next to your skin, it will be a mass of wrinkles by midday. Stick with white and light blue shirts unless you have an extremely well developed fashion sense. Straight collars or button-down collars are the most common collars in

American business. Pin collars make you look pretentious. Cuff links are acceptable in certain fields, such as the financial world on Wall Street, but may cause raised eyebrows elsewhere. Again, the goal is to blend in with your surroundings. Take your cue from others in the organization.

Regardless of what you may think, you can only get one day's wear out of a dress shirt before it needs to be sent to the cleaners. Here's a tip on using dry cleaners: have them use *light* starch. A heavier level of starch will build up on your collars and cause them to shrink temporarily. If your collars are uncomfortably tight even though you haven't gained any weight, starch may be the problem. You can periodically remove the starch by soaking the shirt for an hour in cold water. The investment of a dollar to a dollar-and-a-half to have your shirts professionally cleaned and pressed is a good one.

Suspenders are a little too trendy for most companies. If you do wear them, don't also wear a belt; it makes you look highly insecure. Your belt should match your shoes. If you live in business suits, you can probably invest in a gross of calf-length black socks and never need to worry about the subject of socks again. Make sure your socks go all the way to your calf. Ankle-length socks tend to show off bare skin when you cross your leg—hardly the professional image you're intent on creating.

A final word on socks. Once the elastic on the top gives way, throw the socks away. Nothing looks worse than droopy socks that have collected in a mass around your ankles.

The important point to remember about shoes is that they should be shined and the heels should not be worn down. With the plethora of shoeshine and instant repair shops currently available, there is no excuse for letting your shoes look run-down. Many managers equate scuffed shoes with all sorts of reprehensible behavior. The most conservative shoe to own is a wing tip with laces. Although these shoes are virtually indestructible and will last for decades, you may feel like your grandfather when you wear them. Conservative slip-ons (with *no* flashy gold doodads) are an acceptable alternative.

Own enough pairs of shoes so that you don't have to wear any one pair two days in a row. The leather in shoes needs time to rest between wearings. An investment in three pairs of shoes, which you rotate daily, will last you many years. A single pair of shoes worn daily will only last six months. Don't be penny-wise and pound-foolish.

Black shoes are the most versatile. They go with most any blue or grey suit. Stay away from brown socks, since the only suit they'll go with is brown. If you want to diversify from black, pick a rich-looking cordovan or oxblood shoe. Cordovan goes nicely with your black and grey suits yet adds a little color without looking trendy.

Jewelry should be kept to a minimum. Regardless of how liberal your company, a man wearing an earring is taking a substantial risk with his career. Flashy rings are just that and are best worn during your off-hours. Your watch should be functional and appropriate, not ostentatious. Nothing is more annoying than a person's watch beeping and chiming in a meeting. Make sure your watch is turned off whenever possible.

Advice for Women

Women have a much easier time putting together a wardrobe, since the range of acceptable business attire for women is greater. Fortunately, the days of the severe business suit for women are mostly over. Even in the halls of the most conservative banks and accounting firms, women now wear conservative dresses and shirt-and-jacket combinations. The key is staying conservative. Opt for shades of grey, blue, and earth tones, rather than more attention-getting colors such as red, bright yellow, or lime green. The previous advice for men still applies: look to the next level in the organization for a cue toward acceptable styles.

Women are criticized for dress most often in three areas: perfume, makeup, and jewelry. The rule on jewelry is simple: If you can hear yourself clank, you're wearing too many bracelets. Less is more in business attire. Conservative earrings, a necklace, and one ring per hand are general guidelines to follow.

Be careful about how much perfume you wear. Today's offices tend to be small. You don't want the office to still have the smell of Chanel fifteen minutes after you've left. Since your senses quickly adapt to the perfume you're wearing, it's easy to apply too much. Also, be careful about how much makeup you apply. Makeup can enhance your professionalism, or it can draw attention to your makeup.

Although you might wish it to be otherwise, your image is extremely important in establishing credibility within the organization. Your goal should be to blend in with those whom you wish to impress. Thus, look to the next level in the organization for clues on what constitutes appropriate business attire in your company. In order for your efforts at negotiating to be taken seriously, *you* must be taken seriously. The image you project plays a large part in that perception.

Managing Reference Checks

Your success in salary negotiating depends on your convincing the company of the value you bring to the organization. While your interviewing and communication skills are critical for success, don't overlook the role that your references will play in the process. The company will undoubtedly want to take more than just your word for how good you are. Unfortunately, people don't often appreciate the important role that their references play.

Assuring Your
References Know You

The vice-president of a marketing consulting firm related the following unfortunate story to me. He received a telephone call one morning from the employment manager of a large midwestern consumer goods company. The employment manager said that the vice-president had been named as a reference by an individual who the consumer goods company had under consideration for a job. Would he be willing to discuss the circumstances under which he knew the candidate? Normally the vice-president would have been delighted, except in this instance he could not recall who the individual was. The impression this left upon the employment manager can well be imagined.

Not informing individuals that you are giving their names as references, or not prepping them on what you would like them to say about you, is an often overlooked step of the negotiation process. Mishandling references can cause real problems that could otherwise be avoided. Although it seems obvious, many individuals don't take the extra step of discussing their goals and objectives with the people they intend to use as references. Doing so is well worth the effort. Let's examine how you can maintain control over the reference check process and use it to your maximum advantage.

The Right Number

How many references do you need? You should be prepared to provide four to six individuals who can speak about your professional, technical, or managerial capabilities. These might include supervisors, co-workers, vendors, or customers. They should all be prepared to speak about you from a business perspective. Individuals who can only attest to your fine moral fiber are of less interest to future bosses.

If you are a recent college graduate with little work experience, teachers and professors are suitable alternatives to employers. However, try to include only those teachers that really know you. Employers will not be impressed with a professor whose only comment is, "According to my records, Tina received an A in my class."

Tread equally carefully in the use of celebrities or famous personalities. Bosses look at these references with a great deal of skepticism. However, if you have established connections with individuals who are highly regarded in your particular industry, their recommendation can carry great weight and help increase your value in the employer's estimation.

Coaching

You must prep your references on what you want them to say about you. First, you should discuss the type of job you are applying for. Next, talk about those aspects of your previous experience that most relate to the requirements of the prospective assignment. Ask your references if they feel comfortable discussing your background in a particular area. Give your references examples of when you demonstrated a particular skill which you think would be of interest to the recruiter. In order to provide such examples, you will have had to research the company extensively and have made educated assumptions about the skills the company is looking for. You'll be pleased when you learn that the anecdotes your references cited to the recruiter were the same ones you discussed in preparation. Far too often job seekers leave this aspect of using references to chance.

Thank your references for the role they are playing in your negotiations and include them in your list of people receiving periodic updates on your effort. You will find that most people are flattered to be asked to serve as a reference and are very interested in the success of your research. Don't forget to ask your references for ideas and feedback. These individuals are often invaluable networking contacts.

Your references may be asked to provide the names of other people who can speak about your skills. Discuss this in advance with your references. Suggest names of other individuals that the reference might give if asked. It is important that you maintain control over the reference-checking process.

Will your references be called? No precise data has been collected on this question, yet anecdotal feedback from recruiters indicates that it is unlikely all of the provided references will be called. However, it's impossible to predict which of your references will be contacted, so it's best to make sure that all your references are prepped in the manner discussed.

Should You Accept a Salary Cut?

Should you ever accept a lower base salary in a new position? This is a question confronting more and more job changers. While there are no simple answers, since each person's case is unique, there are compelling reasons both for and against accepting a lower salary.

Know the Market, and Your Value

Making the right salary decision is dependent upon first knowing your market value. As discussed earlier, there are a number of methods to determine this value. Co-workers are often a valuable source of information, although it is important to differentiate between what your co-workers think they should be making and true market value. Two more impartial sources are executive recruiting firms and university placement offices. Since executive recruiters earn their livelihood by keeping their finger on the pulse of the employment marketplace, they are a particularly valuable resource. When discussing your compensation with a recruiter, make sure that the recruiter specializes in your field. Some of the larger firms, such as accounting recruiter Robert Half Inc., periodically publish salary surveys that are available upon request.

Accepting a lower salary may be inevitable if you are a victim of a layoff from a large corporation and you can't leave the area. The salary scales for larger companies are often considerably higher than those for smaller employers. If you are restricted geographically and smaller employers are your most likely source of future employment, a lower salary unfortunately is a possible outcome.

The decision to accept a lower salary often makes sense if you are changing careers. In most cases, compensation directly relates to the amount of experience you have in a particular field. Walking away from your career equity by changing careers will normally result in your being paid less money. The reality of a lower salary is the ultimate test on how committed you are to changing professions. For some people, this financial sacrifice is worth it.

Consider the Whole Package

Finally, accepting a lower salary makes sense in situations where you can receive some other additional form of compensation. An example might be where you take a smaller salary in exchange for an equity or ownership opportunity with a new employer. Individuals pursuing sales or marketing positions often work for a small base salary but have the potential to earn a substantial total compensation through bonuses and commissions. If you are considering such an opportunity, make sure you fully understand how the bonuses are computed and how much individuals with backgrounds similar to yours have earned in their first year.

It certainly doesn't make sense to accept less money if you are currently employed and being actively recruited by another company. If you are in this enviable position, you can expect for the competing firm to make it worth your while to change jobs. Keep in mind that you are in a strong negotiating position and that it seldom pays to compromise too early.

In fact, compromising too early on salary is one of the major sources of ultimate frustration for many job changers. While one should not have unrealistic salary expectations, and although compromise is a common element to the salary negotiation process, candidates often sell themselves short. This is particularly true of individuals who have been affected by a layoff. Since being laid off can greatly impact one's self-esteem, an unfortunate response to this event is to settle for less money than one can legitimately command in the marketplace. In these situations, as one settles into the new job and the financial compromise becomes economic reality, a great deal of job dissatisfaction can result. This often ultimately affects job performance and can prove disastrous.

The key to determining what salary is right for you depends first on knowing your market value. Be realistic, but don't compromise too quickly. Only you can determine if it makes good sense to accept a lower salary in a new assignment.

VGM CAREER BOOKS

OPPORTUNITIES IN
*Available in both paperback and
  hardbound editions*
Accounting
Acting
Advertising
Aerospace
Agriculture
Airline
Animal and Pet Care
Architecture
Automotive Service
Banking
Beauty Culture
Biological Sciences
Biotechnology
Book Publishing
Broadcasting
Building Construction Trades
Business Communication
Business Management
Cable Television
Carpentry
Chemical Engineering
Chemistry
Child Care
Chiropractic Health Care
Civil Engineering
Cleaning Service
Commercial Art and Graphic Design
Computer Aided Design and
  Computer Aided Mfg.
Computer Maintenance
Computer Science
Counseling & Development
Crafts
Culinary
Customer Service
Dance
Data Processing
Dental Care
Direct Marketing
Drafting
Electrical Trades
Electronic and Electrical Engineering
Electronics
Energy
Engineering
Engineering Technology
Environmental
Eye Care
Fashion
Fast Food
Federal Government
Film
Financial
Fire Protection Services
Fitness
Food Services
Foreign Language
Forestry
Gerontology
Government Service
Graphic Communications
Health and Medical
High Tech
Home Economics
Hospital Administration
Hotel & Motel Management
Human Resources Management
  Careers
Information Systems
Insurance
Interior Design
International Business
Journalism
Laser Technology
Law

Law Enforcement and Criminal Justice
Library and Information Science
Machine Trades
Magazine Publishing
Management
Marine & Maritime
Marketing
Materials Science
Mechanical Engineering
Medical Technology
Metalworking
Microelectronics
Military
Modeling
Music
Newspaper Publishing
Nursing
Nutrition
Occupational Therapy
Office Occupations
Opticiany
Optometry
Packaging Science
Paralegal Careers
Paramedical Careers
Part-time & Summer Jobs
Performing Arts
Petroleum
Pharmacy
Photography
Physical Therapy
Physician
Plastics
Plumbing & Pipe Fitting
Podiatric Medicine
Postal Service
Printing
Property Management
Psychiatry
Psychology
Public Health
Public Relations
Purchasing
Real Estate
Recreation and Leisure
Refrigeration and Air Conditioning
Religious Service
Restaurant
Retailing
Robotics
Sales
Sales & Marketing
Secretarial
Securities
Social Science
Social Work
Speech-Language Pathology
Sports & Athletics
Sports Medicine
State and Local Government
Teaching
Technical Communications
Telecommunications
Television and Video
Theatrical Design & Production
Transportation
Travel
Trucking
Veterinary Medicine
Visual Arts
Vocational and Technical
Warehousing
Waste Management
Welding
Word Processing
Writing
Your Own Service Business

CAREERS IN Accounting; Advertising;
Business; Communications; Computers;
Education; Engineering; Health Care;
High Tech; Law; Marketing; Medicine;
Science

CAREER DIRECTORIES
Careers Encyclopedia
Dictionary of Occupational Titles
Occupational Outlook Handbook

CAREER PLANNING
Admissions Guide to Selective
  Business Schools
Career Planning and Development for
  College Students and Recent
  Graduates
Careers Checklists
Careers for Animal Lovers
Careers for Bookworms
Careers for Culture Lovers
Careers for Foreign Language
  Aficionados
Careers for Good Samaritans
Careers for Gourmets
Careers for Nature Lovers
Careers for Numbers Crunchers
Careers for Sports Nuts
Careers for Travel Buffs
Guide to Basic Resume Writing
Handbook of Business and
  Management Careers
Handbook of Health Care Careers
Handbook of Scientific and
  Technical Careers
How to Change Your Career
How to Choose the Right Career
How to Get and Keep
  Your First Job
How to Get into the Right Law School
How to Get People to Do Things
  Your Way
How to Have a Winning Job Interview
How to Land a Better Job
How to Make the Right Career Moves
How to Market Your College Degree
How to Prepare a *Curriculum Vitae*
How to Prepare for College
How to Run Your Own Home Business
How to Succeed in Collge
How to Succeed in High School
How to Write a Winning Resume
Joyce Lain Kennedy's Career Book
Planning Your Career of Tomorrow
Planning Your College Education
Planning Your Military Career
Planning Your Young Child's
  Education
Resumes for Advertising Careers
Resumes for College Students & Recent
  Graduates
Resumes for Communications Careers
Resumes for Education Careers
Resumes for High School Graduates
Resumes for High Tech Careers
Resumes for Sales and Marketing Careers
Successful Interviewing for College
  Seniors

SURVIVAL GUIDES
Dropping Out or Hanging In
High School Survival Guide
College Survival Guide

VGM Career Horizons
a division of *NTC Publishing Group*
4255 West Touhy Avenue
Lincolnwood, Illinois 60646-1975